MW01056162

PURIFICATION OF THE HEART

Purification of the Heart

SIGNS, SYMPTOMS, AND CURES OF THE SPIRITUAL DISEASES OF THE HEART

Translation and Commentary of Imam al-Mawlūds' Maṭharat al-Qulūb

Hamza Yusuf

SANDALA

Published by Sandala, Inc, 2012
www.sandala.org
info@sandala.org

Revised edition.

Printed in the United States of America.
ISBN-10: 098556590
ISBN-13: 978-0-9855659-0-9

Cover Photography: Peter Sanders
Cover Design and Layout: Abdallateef Whiteman
Managing Editor: Uzma Husaini

Contents

بسم الله الرحمن الرحيم

Acknowledgments

On the Day of Judgment no one is safe save the one who returns to God with a pure heart. (QUR'AN)

Surely in the breasts of humanity is a lump flesh, if sound then the whole body is sound, and if corrupt then the whole body is corrupt. Is it not the heart? (Prophet Muhammad ﷺ)

Blessed are the pure at heart, for they shall see God. (Jesus عليه السلام)

"Whoever has not thanked people, has not thanked God," said the Prophet Muhammad ﷺ.This work is the result of the collaboration of many people. I am honored to have studied the meanings of this poem with my friend and pure-hearted teacher Abdallah ould Ahmadna. I also thank the eminent scholar and spiritual master, Shaykh Muhammad Hasan ould al-Khadim, for giving me license to teach and translate the poem and whose outstanding commentary on it was my constant companion during the classes and remains so today. Thank you, Feraidoon Mojadedi, for your continued love and support and for having the zeal to organize the classes and the small, blessed school that would become Zaytuna. More gratitude than can be expressed goes to Dr. Hisham al-Alusi, who humbly sat on the floor against the window to attend the original classes that would become this text. He saw from the start the importance of this work and, through his extraordinary efforts, helped realize more than I had hoped to with the Zaytuna Institute and now Zaytuna College. I also thank my sister Nabila, who has worked tirelessly through Alhambra Productions (now Sandala, Inc.) and Kinza Academy to spread this message. I'm grateful to Hisham Mahmoud for his careful editing of the translation of the poem, and to my friend and artist Abdullateef Whiteman for his beautiful design of the cover. I am also deeply thankful and appreciative to all those who worked diligently on the transcription, proofreading and editing of the text. Finally, my immense gratitude goes to the mother of my children, Liliana, whose pure heart is fortunate enough not to need the contents of this book.

Note to the Reader

I OFFER THIS book to you, the reader, in the spirit of gratitude just as I was taught this text years ago by my teacher, Abdallah ould Ahmadna in a similar spirit - gratitude and thankfulness to our Lord. The purpose of this book, is not, and has never been, for commercial gain, but to help us all along the path of purification, so we can serve humanity, and ultimately God, in the best of ways. In an age where dignity, nobility, and honor have become ideals of the past, it is my sincere hope that works like this may help rekindle the desire for self-improvement and introspection in all of us.

Staying true to this principle, the publishers and I have chosen a Creative Commons copyright, which allows sharing of this book for non-commercial purposes. Portions or excerpts may be scanned or photocopied for use on internet mediums or written works, as long it is not sold or used for material gains or profit.

We, at Sandala, ask in return that you keep us in your prayers and give appropriate credit for the work wherever you may use it. This credit is only so people can choose to help support more of our publishing initiatives. Proceeds from any sales of this book will be utilized for further educational projects and productions. It is our deepest desire to present our sacred tradition in the most dignified of ways, as it deserves, while maintaining affordability and accessibility. Anyone who cannot meet the costs may contact the publishing house, Sandala Inc., and we will be happy and honored to gift them this book or any of our other products.

Such is the essence of our tradition, *shukr* (gratitude). Just as the Prophet Muhammad ﷺ said to Lady ʿĀishah ؓ in the midst of his late night prayers, "Should I not be a thankful servant?", so too do we hope to always return to the station of gratitude in all of our affairs.

If you are thankful, surely I will increase you. (QUR'AN, 14:7)

HAMZA YUSUF
Sandala, Inc.

Translator's Introduction

ALMOST UNIVERSALLY, RELIGIOUS traditions have stressed the importance of the condition of the heart. In the Muslim scripture, the Day of Judgment is described as, "*a day in which neither wealth nor children shall be of any benefit [to anyone], except one who comes to God with a sound heart* (QUR'AN, 26:88-89)." The sound heart is understood to be free of character defects and spiritual blemishes. This "heart" is actually the spiritual heart and not the physical organ per se, although in Islamic tradition the spiritual heart is centered in the physical. One of the extraordinary aspects of the modern era is that we are discovering aspects about the heart unknown in previous times, although there were remarkable insights in ancient traditions. For instance, according to traditional Chinese medicine, the heart houses what is known as *shen*, which is *spirit*. The Chinese characters for thinking, thought, love, the intention to listen, and virtue all contain the ideogram for the heart.

In nearly every culture in the world, people use metaphors that directly or indirectly allude to the heart. We call certain types of people "hard-hearted," usually because they show no mercy and kindness. Likewise, people are said to have "cold hearts" and others yet who are "warm-hearted." We speak of people as wearing their "hearts on their sleeves" because they do not (or cannot) conceal their emotions from others. When someone's words or actions penetrate our souls and affect us profoundly, we say that this person "touched my heart" or "touched the core of my being." The Arabic equivalent for the English word *core* (which originally in Latin meant *heart*) is known as *lubb*, which also refers to the heart, as well as the intellect and the essence of something.

The most ancient Indo-European word for heart means "that which leaps," which is consonant with the idea of the beating heart that leaps in the breast of man. People speak of their hearts as "leaping for joy." People also say that their heart "skipped a beat" when they come upon something startling that elicited from them a very strong emotional response. When people fall in love, they speak of "stealing one's heart." There are many other metaphors involving the human heart, owing to its centrality in life. These phrases— however casually we may utter them today—have roots in ancient concepts.

The ancients were aware of spiritual diseases of the heart. And this understanding is certainly at the essence of Islamic teachings. The Qur'an defines three types of people: *al-mu'minūn* (believers), *al-kāfirūn* (scoffers or atheists), and *al-munāfiqūn* (hypocrites). The believers are described as people whose hearts are alive and full of light, while the scoffers are in darkness: *Is one who was dead and then We revived [with faith] and made for him a light by which to walk among the people like one who is in darkness from which he cannot exit?* (QUR'AN, 6:122). According to commentators of the Qur'an, "*the one who was dead*" refers to having a dead heart, which God revived with the light of guidance that one may walk straight and honorably among human beings. Also, the Prophet Muhammad ﷺ said, "The difference between the one who remembers God and one who does not is like the difference between the living and the dead." In essence, the believer is someone whose heart is alive, while the disbeliever is someone whose heart is spiritually dead. The hypocrite, however, is somebody whose heart is diseased. The Qur'an speaks of certain people with diseased hearts (self-inflicted, we understand) and, as a result, they were increased in their disease (QUR'AN, 2:10).

The heart is centered slightly to the left of our bodies. Two sacred languages of Arabic and Hebrew are written from right to left, toward the heart, which, as some have noted, mirrors the purpose of writing, namely to affect the heart. One should also consider the ritual of circumambulation or circling around the Ancient House (or Kaʿba) in Mecca during the Pilgrimage. It is performed in a counterclockwise fashion, with the left side of the worshipper facing the House—with the heart inclined towards it to remind us of God and His presence in the life of humanity.

The physical heart, which houses the spiritual heart, beats about

100,000 times a day, pumping two gallons of blood per minute and over 100 gallons per hour. If one were to attempt to carry 100 gallons of water (whose density is lighter than blood) from one place to another, it would be an exhausting task. Yet the human heart does this every hour of every day for an entire lifetime without respite. The vascular system transporting life-giving blood is over 60,000 miles long—more than two times the circumference of the earth. So when we conceive of our blood being pumped throughout our bodies, know that this means that it travels through 60,000 miles of a closed vascular system that connects all the parts of the body—all the vital organs and living tissues—to this incredible heart.

We now know that the heart starts beating before the brain is fully fashioned, that is, without the benefit of a fully formed central nervous system. The dominant theory states that the central nervous system is what controls the entire human being, with the brain as its center. Yet we also know that the nervous system does not initiate the beat of the heart, but that it is actually self-initiated, or, as we would say, initiated by God. We also know that the heart, should all of its connections to the brain be severed (as they are during a heart transplant), continues to beat.

Many in the West have long proffered that the brain is the center of consciousness. But in traditional Islamic thought—as in other traditions—the heart is viewed as the center of our being. The Qur'an, for example, speaks of wayward people who have hearts "*with which they do not understand* (QUR'AN, 7:179)." Also the Qur'an mentions people who mocked the Prophet ﷺ and were entirely insincere in listening to his message, so God "*placed over their hearts a covering that they may not understand it and in their ears [He placed] acute deafness* (QUR'AN 6:25)." Their inability to understand is a deviation from the spiritual function of a sound heart, just as their ears have been afflicted with a spiritual "*deafness*". So we understand from this that the center of the intellect, the center of human consciousness and conscience, is actually the heart and not the brain. Only recently have we discovered that there are over 40,000 neurons in the heart. In other words, there are cells in the heart that are communicating with the brain. While the brain sends messages to the heart, the heart also sends messages to the brain.

Two physiologists in the 1970s, John and Beatrice Lacey, conducted a study and found that the brain sent messages to the heart, but the heart did not automatically obey the messages. Sometimes the heart sped up, while at other times it slowed down, indicating that the heart itself has its own type of intelligence. The brain receives signals from the heart through the brain's amygdala, thalamus, and cortex. The amygdala relates to emotions, while the cortex or the neocortex relates to learning and reasoning. Although this interaction is something that is not fully understood from a physiological point of view, we do know that the heart is an extremely sophisticated organ with secrets still veiled from us.

The Prophet of Islam ﷺ spoke of the heart as a repository of knowledge and a vessel sensitive to the deeds of the body. He said, for example, that wrongdoing irritates the heart. So the heart actually perceives wrong action. In fact, when people do terrible things, the core of their humanity is injured. Fyodor Dostoyevsky expresses brilliantly in *Crime and Punishment* that the crime itself is the punishment because human beings ultimately have to live with the painful consequences of their deeds. When someone commits a crime, he does so first against his own heart, which then affects the whole human being. The person enters a state of spiritual agitation and often tries to suppress it. The root meaning of the word *kufr* (disbelief) is *to cover* something up. As it relates to this discussion, the problems we see in our society come down to covering up or suppressing the symptoms of its troubles. The agents used to do this include alcohol, drugs, sexual experimentation and deviance, power grabs, wealth, arrogance, pursuit of fame, and the like. These enable people to submerge themselves into a state of heedlessness concerning their essential nature. People work very hard to cut themselves off from their hearts and the natural feelings found there. The pressures to do this are very strong in our modern culture.

One of the major drawbacks of being severed from the heart is that the more one is severed, the sicker the heart becomes, for the heart needs nourishment. Heedlessness starves the heart, robs it of its spiritual manna. One enters into a state of unawareness—a debilitating lack of awareness of God and an acute neglect of humanity's ultimate destination: the infinite world of the Hereafter. When one peers into the limitless world through remembrance of God and increases in beneficial knowledge, one's concerns become more focused on the infinite world, not the finite one that is disappearing and ephemeral. When people are completely immersed in the material world, believing that this world is all that matters and all that exists and that they are not accountable for their actions, they affect a spiritual death of their hearts. Before the heart dies, however, it shows symptoms of affliction. These afflictions are the spiritual diseases of the heart (the center of our being)—the topic of this book.

In Islamic tradition, these diseases fall under two categories. The first is known as *shubuhāt* or *obfuscations*. These are diseases that relate to impaired or inappropriate understanding. For instance, if somebody is fearful that God will not provide for him or her, this is considered a disease of the heart because a sound heart has knowledge and trust, not doubt and anxiety. The category of *shubuhāt* alludes to aspects closely connected to the heart: the soul, the ego, Satan's whisperings and instigations, caprice, and the ardent love of this ephemeral world. The heart is an organ designed to be in a state of calm, which is achieved with the remembrance of God: *Most surely, in the remembrance of God do hearts find calm* (QUR'AN, 13:28). This calm is what the heart seeks out and gravitates to. It yearns always to remember God the Exalted. But when God is not remembered, when human beings forget God, then the heart falls into a state of agitation and turmoil. In this state it becomes vulnerable to diseases because it is undernourished and cut off. Cells require oxygen, so we breathe. If we stop breathing, we die. The heart also needs to breathe, and the breath of the heart is none other than the remembrance of God. Without it, the spiritual heart dies. The very purpose of revelation and of scripture is to remind us that our hearts need to be nourished.

We enter the world in a state the Qur'an calls *fiṭrah*, our original state and inherent nature that is disposed to accept faith and prefer morality. But we soon learn anxiety mainly from our parents and then our societies. The heart is created vulnerable to anxiety and agitation (QUR'AN, 70:19). Those who are protected from this state are people of prayer; people who establish prayer and guard its performance with a humble and open heart connected with God, the Lord of all creation. The highest ranks among people are those who do not allow anything to divert them from the remembrance of God. They are the ones who remember God as they are "*standing, sitting, and reclining on their sides* (QUR'AN, 3:191)."

The second category of disease concerns the base desires of the self and is called *shahawāt*. This relates to our desires exceeding their natural state, as when people live merely to satisfy these urges and are led by them. Islam provides the method by which our hearts can become sound and safe again. This method has been the subject of brilliant and insightful scholarship for centuries in the Islamic tradition. One can say that Islam in essence is a program to restore purity and calm to the heart through the remembrance of God.

This present text is based on the poem known as *Maṭharat al-Qulūb* (literally, *Purification of the Hearts*), which offers the means by which purification can be achieved. It is a treatise on the "alchemy of the hearts," namely, a manual on how to transform the heart. It was written by a great scholar and saint, Shaykh Muḥammad Mawlūd al-Yaʿqūbī al-Musawī al-Muratānī. As his name indicates, he was from Mauritania in West Africa. He was a master of all the Islamic sciences, including the inward sciences of the heart. He stated that he wrote this poem because he observed the prevalence of diseased hearts. He saw students of religion spending their time learning abstract sciences that people were not really in need of, to the neglect of those sciences that pertain to what people are accountable for in the next life, namely, the spiritual condition of the heart. In one of his most cited statements, the Prophet ﷺ said, "Actions are based upon intentions." All deeds are thus valued according to the intentions behind them, and intentions emanate from the heart. So every action a person intends or performs is rooted in the heart.

Imam Mawlūd realized that the weakness of society was a matter of weakness of character in the heart. Imam Mawlūd based his text on many previous illustrious works, especially Imam al-Ghazalī's great *Iḥyā' ʿUlūm al-Dīn (The Revivification of the Sciences of the Religion)*. Each of the 40 books of *Iḥyā' ʿUlūm al-Dīn* has the underlying objective of rectifying the human heart.

If we examine the trials and tribulations, wars and other conflicts, every act of injustice all over earth, we'll find they are rooted in human hearts. Covetousness, the desire to aggress and exploit, the longing to pilfer natural resources, the inordinate love of wealth and position, and other maladies are manifestations of diseases found nowhere but in the heart. Every criminal, miser, abuser, scoffer, embezzler, and hateful person does what he or she does because of a diseased heart. If hearts were sound, these actions would no longer be a reality. So if we want to change our world, we do not begin by rectifying the outward. Instead, we must change the condition of our inward. Everything we see happening outside of us is in reality coming from the unseen world within. It is from the unseen world that the phenomenal world emerges, and it is from the unseen realm of our hearts that all actions spring.

The well-known civil rights activist Martin Luther King, Jr. said that in order for people to condemn injustice, they must go through four stages. The first stage is that people must ascertain that indeed injustices are being perpetrated. In his case, it was injustices against African Americans in the United States. The second stage is to negotiate, that is, approach the oppressor and demand justice. If the oppressor refuses, King said that the third stage is self-purification, which starts with the question: "Are we ourselves wrongdoers? Are we ourselves oppressors?" The fourth stage, then, is to take action after true self-examination, after removing one's own wrongs before demanding justice from others.

We of the modern world are reluctant to ask ourselves—when we look at the terrible things that are happening—"Why do they occur?" And if we ask that with all sincerity, the answer will come resoundingly: "All of this is from your own selves." In so many ways, we have brought this upon ourselves. This is the only empowering position we can take. The Qur'an implies that if a people oppress others, God will send another people to oppress them: *We put some oppressors over other oppressors because of what their own hands have earned* (QUR'AN, 6:129). According to Fakhruddīn al-Rāzī (a 12th century scholar of the Qur'an) the verse means that the existence of oppression on earth may be caused by previous oppression. By implication, often the victims of aggression were once aggressors themselves. This, however, is not the case with tribulations, for there are times in which people are indeed tried, but if they respond with patience and perseverance, God will always give them relief and victory. If we examine the life of the Prophet ﷺ in Mecca, it's clear that he and the community of believers were being harmed and oppressed, but they were patient and God gave them victory. Within 23 years, the Prophet ﷺ was not only free of oppression, but became the leader of the entire Arabian Peninsula. Those people who once oppressed him now sought mercy from him; and he was most gracious and kind in his response. Despite their former brutality toward him, the Prophet ﷺ forgave them and admitted them into the brotherhood of faith.

This is the difference between someone whose heart is purified and sound and one whose heart is impure and corrupt. Impure people oppress, and the pure-hearted not only forgive their oppressors, but elevate them in status and character. In order to purify ourselves, we must begin to recognize this truth. This is what this book is all about—a book of self-purification and a manual of liberation. If we work on our hearts, if we actually implement what is suggested here, we'll begin to see changes in our lives, our condition, our society, and even within our own family dynamics. It is a blessing that we have this science of purification, a blessing that this teaching exists in the world today. What remains is for us to take these teachings seriously.

So let us go through what is explained here by this great scholar and learn of the diseases of the heart, examine their etiology (their causes), their signs and symptoms, and, finally, how to treat them. There are two types of treatments: the theoretical treatment, which is understanding the disease itself, and the practical treatment, which focuses on the prescriptions we must take in order to restore the heart's natural purity. If we apply the techniques that have been learned and transmitted by the great scholars of the vast tradition of Islam, we will see results. But just like medicinal prescriptions, the physician cannot force you to take it. The knowledgeable scholars of spiritual purification have given us the treatment, as they have gleaned it from the teachings of the Qur'an and the exemplary model of the Prophet. The teachings are available. They are clear, and they work. It is then up to us to learn and apply them to ourselves and share them with others.

HAMZA YUSUF

Transliteration Key

THE TRANSLITERATION CONVENTION used throughout this book represents the Arabic script as follows:

Consonants:

ء	'	د	d	ض	ḍ	ك	k
ب	b	ذ	dh	ط	ṭ	ل	l
ت	t	ر	r	ظ	ẓ	م	m
ث	th	ز	z	ع	ʿ	ن	n
ج	j	س	s	غ	gh	هـ	h
ح	ḥ	ش	sh	ف	f	و	w
خ	kh	ص	ṣ	ق	q	ي	y

Short vowels:	ـَ	a	ـُ	u	ـِ	i
Long vowels:	ـَا	ā	ـُو	ū	ـِي	ī
Dipthongs:	ـَو	aw	ـَي	ay		

The definite article is rendered *al-* to preserve the representation of the Arabic script as written, not as pronounced, except where fully inflected expressions are quoted as such. Therefore, *ash-shams* is rendered *al-shams*, unless it appears in a fully inflected verbal expression, such as *wa sh-shamsi wa ḍuḥāhā*. Without inflection, this written expression is rendered *wa al-shams wa ḍuḥāhā*.

The *tā' marbūṭah* is represented by a final *h*, unless it ends the first term of an *iḍāfah* construction, as in *laylat al-qadr*. Note that the *tā' marbūṭah* in *ahl al-sunnah wa al-jamāʿah*, for instance, is represented as an *h* because it is not the first term of an *iḍāfah* construction.

Hamzat al-waṣl will only be accounted for whenever preceded by a preposition, never for the definite article *alif-lām*, and will in such cases be indicated by a hyphen. Hence, the phrase *wa-mnun ʿalaynā minnata l-karīmi* indicates *hamzat al-waṣl* with a hyphen in *wa-mnun*, but not in *minnata l-karīmi*.

Words that have entered the English language, such as "hadith," "fatwa," and "imam," are not transliterated or italicized unless rendered in formulaic Arabic expressions or idiomatic phrases.

ﷺ An invocation of God's blessings and peace upon the Prophet Muḥammad: "May God's blessings and peace be upon him."

عليه السلام An invocation of God's peace upon a prophet or angel: "May peace be upon him."

عليهما السلام An invocation of God's peace upon two prophets: "May peace be upon them."

عليهم السلام An invocation of God's peace upon three or more prophets: "May peace be upon them."

رضي الله عنه An invocation of God's contentment with a male companion of the Prophet: "May God be pleased with him."

رضي الله عنها An invocation of God's contentment with a female companion of the Prophet: "May God be pleased with her."

رضي الله عنهما An invocation of God's contentment with two companions of the Prophet: "May God be pleased with them."

رضي الله عنهم An invocation of God's contentment with three or more companions of the Prophet: "May God be pleased with them."

Introduction to Purification

POEM VERSES 1–8

I begin by starting with the heart of beginnings,
for it is the highest and noblest of beginnings.

Have courtesy with God, the High and the Majestic,
by practicing modesty and humility—

Dejected out of shame and humility
humbled in awe, imploring Him—

By giving up your designs for His,
emptied of covetousness for what His servants have,

By hastening to fulfill His commands, and by being wary
of the subtle encroachment of bad manners.

If you—the spiritual aspirant—realize your attributes of servitude,
you will then be assisted with something of the attributes
of the Eternally Besought.

Realize your abject character and impoverishment, and you will
gain dignity and wealth from the All-Powerful.

There is no salvation like the heart's salvation,
given that all the limbs [and organs] respond to its desires.

Courtesy: the Heart of Purification

Imam Mawlūd begins his Arabic didactic poem with a play on words that is lost in translation. "Beginning" in Arabic is *bad'u*, and the word for "heart" (*qalb*) also means, "to reverse something." Reversing the letters in the word *bad'u* results in the word *adab*, which is the term for "courtesy"—and that is where this treatise begins, since courtesy is the portal to the purification of the heart.

Adab in Arabic holds several meanings, in addition to "courtesy." *Adīb* (a derivative of *adab*), for example, has come to mean "an erudite person, someone who is learned," as high manners and courtesy are associated with learning and erudition. However, the idea of courtesy is firmly established at the root of the word *adab*. Imam Mawlūd starts his treatise with courtesy, since excellent behavior and comportment are the doorkeepers to the science of spiritual purification. One must have courtesy with regard to God—behave properly with respect to His presence—if he or she wishes to purify the heart. But how does one achieve this courtesy? Imam Mawlūd mentions two requisite qualities associated with courtesy: modesty (*ḥayā'*) and humility (*dhul*).

Ḥayā', in Arabic, conveys the meaning of "shame," though the root word of *ḥayā'* is closely associated with "life" and "living." The Prophet ﷺ stated, "Every religion has a quality that is characteristic of that religion, and the characteristic of my religion is *ḥayā'*," an internal sense of shame that includes bashfulness and modesty.

As children, many of us had someone say to us at times, "Shame on you!" Unfortunately, shame has now come to be viewed as a negative word, as if it were a pejorative. Parents are now often advised to never cause a child to feel shame. The current wisdom largely suggests that adults should always make the child feel good, regardless of his or her behavior. However, doing so eventually disables naturally occurring deterrents to misbehavior.

Some anthropologists divide cultures into shame cultures and guilt cultures. According to this perspective, shame is an outward mechanism, and guilt is an inward one which alludes to a human mechanism that produces strong feelings of remorse when someone has done something wrong, to the point that he or she needs to rectify the matter.

Most primitive cultures are not guilt-based but are shame-based, which is rooted in the fear of bringing shame upon oneself and the larger family. Islam honors the concept of shame and takes it to another level altogether—to a rank in which one feels a sense of shame before God. When a person acknowledges and realizes that God is fully aware of all that one does, says, and thinks, shame is elevated to a higher plane, to the unseen world from which there is no cover. At this level, one feels a sense of shame even before the angels. So while Muslims comprise a shame-based culture, this notion transcends feeling shame before one's family—whether one's elders or parents—and admits a mechanism that is not subject to the changing norms of human cultures. It is associated with the knowledge and active awareness that God is all-seeing of what one does—a reality that is permanent. The nurturing of this realization in a person deters one from engaging in acts that are displeasing and vulgar. This is the nobility of prophetic teachings.

Imam Mawlūd also mentions that one should have *dhul*, which literally means, "being lowly, abject, or humbled." The Qur'an mentions that people who incur the anger of God have this state of humiliation thrust upon them. This humility or humbleness assumed before God is required for courtesy. Interestingly, the word *munkasiran* is translated as "dejected," though it literally means, "broken." It conveys a sense of being humbled in the majestic presence of God. It refers to the awesome realization that each of us, at every moment, lives and acts before the august presence of the Creator of the heavens and the earth, the one God besides whom there is no power or might in all the universe.

When we seriously reflect on God's perfect watch over His creation and the countless blessings He sends down, and then consider the kind of deeds we bring before Him, what can we possibly feel except humility and shame? These strong feelings should lead us to implore God to change our state, make our desires consonant with His pleasure, giving up our designs for God's designs. This is pure courtesy with respect to God, a requisite for spiritual purification.

The Prophet ﷺ said, "None of you [fully] believes until his desires are in accordance with what I have brought." Being aligned and at peace with the teachings of the Prophet ﷺ, which embody the legacy of the prophetic teachings of Noah, Abraham, Moses, and Jesus عليهم السلام, entails striving to free oneself of greed and refusing the ethic of doing something for an ulterior motive that is essentially selfish and dissonant with the teachings of God's prophets عليهم السلام. A person should not seek anything from God's servants. If one wants anything, one should seek it from God, the Sovereign of the heavens and the earth. The basic rule is to ask God and then work; that is, one should utilize the means (*asbāb*) that one must use in order to achieve something in this world.

Imam Mawlūd then says that one should hasten "to fulfill [God's] command" and be "wary of the subtle encroachment of bad manners," namely, faults that one is unaware of. A hadith states, "One of you will say a word and give it no consideration, though it will drag the person [who uttered it] through Hellfire for 70 years." People often become so disconnected from prophetic teachings that they unwittingly inflict great harm upon themselves. It is comparable to a heedless person who finds himself in diplomatic circles laden with protocol, yet he makes horrendous breaches of protocol without realizing it. With regard to God, the matter is obviously much more serious, as one's soul may be harmed by one's own breaches. In this case, the protocol involves knowledge of God and what He has enjoined and proscribed.

Freedom and Purification

Imam Mawlūd speaks next about freedom, which is achieved when one realizes the qualities of shame and humility, and empties oneself of their opposites (shamelessness and arrogance). With these qualities come true freedom, wealth, and dignity, which require manumission from the bonds of one's whims. People may claim to be "free," yet they cannot control themselves from gluttony in the presence of food or from illicit sexual relations when the opportunity presents itself. Such a notion of freedom is devoid of substance.

Freedom has real meaning when, for example, a situation of temptation arises and one remains God-fearing, steadfast, and in control of one's actions. This holds true even when the temptation produces flickers of desire in a person who nonetheless refrains from indulging. Imam al-Ghazālī speaks at length about the desires of our limbs and organs and refers to the stomach and the genitals as being the two "dominators"; if they are under control, all other aspects of desire are kept in check. The tongue is also a formidable obstacle. There are people, for example, who appear incapable of refraining from backbiting and speaking ill of others, and they often do so without realizing it.

It is common for people to dislike impoverishment or humility because they perceive them as abjectness. Yet the Prophet ﷺ chose poverty over wealth; he did not have money in his home; he did not have jewelry; he slept on the floor upon a bed made of leather that was stuffed with palm fibers; and he had two pillows in his room for guests. In much of today's culture, living this way would be considered extreme poverty. Imam Mawlūd stresses that dignity with God comes to those who are humble before Him, those who place prime value on how they are received by their Maker and not by how they will be judged by the ephemeral norms of people. Dignity and honor are gifts; the Qur'an says about God, "*You exalt whomever You will, and You debase whomever You will*" (3:26). Proofs of this divine law abound. There are many accounts, for example, of people who were once in positions of authority and wealth but now find themselves as paupers, completely stripped of their former glory, reduced, in many instances, to wards of the state. God is powerful over all things, and all good, authority, and provision are in His hand, not ours.

From this, we derive an important principle: if one ignobly pursues an attribute, he or she will be donned with its opposite. God humbles and humiliates the haughty ones, those who arrogantly seek out rank and glory before the eyes of people. The Qur'an gives the examples of Pharaoh and Korah and their abject fall and disgrace. Conversely, if one is humble before God, He will render him or her honorable.

Imam Mawlūd goes on to explain that there is no salvation "like the heart's salvation, given that all the limbs [and organs] respond to its desires." If one's heart is safe, so too are the limbs and organs, for they carry out the deeds inspired by the heart. The limbs and organs of the corrupt become instruments through which corruption is spread, as the Qur'an states: "*Today, We shall set a seal upon their mouths; and their hands will speak to Us and their feet shall bear witness to what they have earned*" (QUR'AN, 36:65); "*And spend [on the needy] in the way of God. And do not throw yourselves into ruin by your own hands*" (Qur'an, 2:195); "*And We shall say, 'Taste the chastisement of burning! That is for what your hands have forwarded [for yourselves]. And God never wrongs [His] servants'*"(Qur'an, 3:181–82); "*They shall have immense torment on the day when their tongues and their hands and their legs bear witness against them for what they had been doing*" (QUR'AN, 24:23–24).

According to a hadith, the tongue is the "interpreter of the heart." Hypocrisy is wretched because the hypocrite says with his tongue what is not in his heart. He wrongs his tongue and oppresses his heart. But if the heart is sound, the condition of the tongue follows suit. We are commanded to be upright in our speech, which is a gauge of the heart's state. According to a prophetic tradition, each morning, when the limbs and organs awaken in the spiritual world, they shudder and say to the tongue, "Fear God concerning us! For if you are upright, then we are upright; and if you deviate, we too deviate." Engaging in the regular remembrance of God (*dhikr*) safeguards the tongue and replaces idle talk with words and phrases that raise one in honor. The tongue is essential in developing courtesy with God, which is the whole point of existence.

POEM VERSES 9–15

After firmly grasping this foundation,
then mastering the heart's infirmities is the second stage,

Knowledge of the heart's ailments, what causes each of
them and what removes them, is an obligation on everyone.

This is the ruling of al-Ghazālī. However, this does not
apply to one who was already granted a sound heart,

As scholars other than al-Ghazālī opine,
for al-Ghazālī reckoned the heart's illnesses as inherent

To humanity. Others deemed them predominant in man—
not qualities necessarily inherent to his nature.
But know that obliteration of these diseases until no trace
remains is beyond the capacity of human beings.

> *Nonetheless, here I give you what you need to know of their definitions, etiologies, and cures.*

The Purification Process

Purifying the heart is a process. First, one must understand the necessity of having courtesy with God and the importance of fulfilling its requirements, as noted above. Second, one must be aware of the diseases of the heart—aware of their existence, their ailments, and the deleterious complications and troubles that ensue from them, and recognize that these diseases prevent one from attaining this courtesy. Knowledge of the diseases of the heart, their causes, and how to remove them is an obligation on every sane adult human being.

Imam Mawlūd cites Imam al-Ghazālī (an eleventh century master scholar of the science of purification) holding the position that it is indeed an obligation on everyone to learn about the ailments of the heart and their cures. Imam Mawlūd then states that some scholars hold that this is not an obligation per se for everyone, particularly for a person who has already been blessed with a sound heart and has been spared these maladies. Imam al-Ghazālī dissents and says that these diseases are inherent to the human condition. One can observe, for example, greed, jealousy, hatred, and the like in children, though the diseases do not necessarily endure. But how does this compare with "Original Sin," the Christian concept which states that people are corrupt by nature?

In short, though Muslim scholars of the caliber of Imam al-Ghazālī do say that diseases of the heart are related to human nature, they would also say that this manifests itself as human inclination. However, Muslims do not believe that this inclination is a result of Adam's wrongdoing or that Adam ﷺ brought upon himself, and transferred to his descendants, a permanent state of sin that can only be lifted by sacrificial blood. Adam and Eve erred, no doubt, but they then turned in penitence to God, and God accepted their repentance and forgave them both. This is the nature of God's forgiveness. There was no blemish passed on to their progeny. The Qur'an declares that no soul bears the burden of sin of another soul (QUR'AN, 6:164). However, this fact does not negate the existence of base instincts among humans.

This matter relates to the fact that the heart is a spiritual organ. The unseen aspect of the heart contains a bad seed that has the potential of becoming like a cancer that can metastasize and overtake the heart. The bacterium responsible for tuberculosis, for example, lives latent in the lungs of millions of people. When its carriers age or succumb to another disease that weakens their immune system, tuberculosis may start to emerge. This analogy illustrates that there is a dormant element in the human heart that, if nurtured and allowed to grow, can damage the soul and eventually destroy it. The Prophet ﷺ stated, "If the son of Adam sins, a black spot appears in the heart. And if the person repents, it is erased. But if he does not, it continues to grow until the whole heart becomes pitch black." (Incidentally, this notion of associating the color black with sin is not racist in its origins. The attribution has been long used, even among black Africans who refer to a person who is wretched as "black-hearted." The Qur'an says about successful people on the Day of Judgment that their "*faces become white*" (3:106). This does not mean "white" as a hue of skin; rather it refers to light and brightness, which are spiritual descriptions not associated with actual color. A black person can have spiritual light in his face, and a white person can have darkness, and vice versa, depending on one's spiritual and moral condition.)

Imam al-Ghazālī considers ailments of the heart to be part of the Adamic potential. He believes one is obliged to know this about human nature in order to be protected. Other scholars simply consider these ailments to be predominant in man; that is, most people have these qualities, but not necessarily everybody.

It is interesting that Imam Mawlūd says it is impossible to rid oneself of these diseases completely. This implies that purification is a lifelong process, not something that is applied once and then forgotten. Purity of heart never survives a passive relationship. One must always guard his or her heart.

There is a well-known hadith which states that every child is born in the state of *fiṭrah*. Many Muslims translate this into English as, "Every child is born a *Muslim*." However, the hadith says, "*fiṭrah*," which means that people are born inclined to faith, with an intuitive awareness of divine purpose and a nature built to receive the prophetic message. What remains then is to nurture one's *fiṭrah* and cultivate this inclination to faith and purity of heart.

Miserliness

POEM VERSES 16–25

Now then: the refusal to give what is obliged according to sacred law or to virtuous merit is the essence of miserliness, which is mentioned [among the diseases of the heart].

As for the obligations of sacred law, they are such things as zakat, supporting one's dependents, rights due to others, and relieving the distressed. Examples of [virtuous merit] include not nitpicking over trivialities.

Avoiding this is even more important with respect to a neighbor, a relative, or a wealthy person;

Or when hosting guests; or concerning something in which such behavior is inappropriate, such as purchasing a burial shroud or a sacrificial animal, or purchasing something you intend to donate to the needy.

Thus one who makes matters difficult for one whose rights clearly render this inappropriate to do so, such as a neighbor, has indeed torn away the veils of dignity. This is as the majestic and guiding sages have stated.

This is comparable to one who fulfills his obligations without good cheer or who spends from the least of what he possesses.

Its root is love of this world for its own sake,
or so that the self can acquire some of its fleeting pleasures.

Definition and Causes

Imam Mawlūd brings to the foreground the definitions of these diseases, their etiology (origins and causes), and how to cure them. The first disease he speaks of is miserliness (*bukhl*). It is first not because it is the worst of characteristics but because of alphabetical ordering in Arabic.

He mentions two aspects of miserliness. One relates to the shariah (sacred law), that is rights due to God and to His creation. The other pertains to *murū'ah*, which is an important Arabic concept that connotes manliness and valor. In pre-Islamic Arab culture, valor was a defining concept. It is similar to Western ideals of chivalry and virtue. (The Latin word *vir* means, "man." Similarly, the Arabic root for "virtue," *murū'ah*, is a cognate of the word for "man"—though scholars state that it refers both to "manliness" and "humanity.")

Regarding the first aspect, the sacred law obliges the payment of zakat, charity distributed to the needy. Miserliness in the form of not giving zakat is explicitly forbidden. The same is true with one's obligation to support his wife and children. Even if a couple suffers a divorce, the man must still pay child support. When it comes to the obligations of sacred law, miserliness is the most virulent form.

In terms of valor, the Imam goes into some detail. One should never create difficulty over paltry matters, he says. When it comes to debt, it is far better for the creditor to be flexible and magnanimous than demanding and unbearable. This is especially true when the creditor is not in need of repayment, while the debtor faces hardship. An understanding and compassionate creditor is one who has valor. Having this quality of magnanimity is not an obligation in sacred law because the creditor has the right to what is owed to him. But if he is apathetic to the needs of the debtor and insists on his payment, this is considered reprehensible.

An Islamic ethic for the wealthy is that they exude magnanimity, generosity, and the demeanor of lenience. A hadith recounts that a wealthy individual would instruct his servants when collecting money on his behalf, "If [the debtors] do not have the means, tell them their debts are absolved." When this wealthy man died without any good deeds save his largesse with debtors, according to the hadith, God said to His angels, "This man was forgiving of people's transgressions against him, and I'm more worthy of forgiving transgressions. Therefore, I forgive him."

When hosting guests, one should not be persnickety, says Imam Mawlūd. For example, if a guest spills something on the carpet, the host should not display anger or, worse yet, scold the guest. It is far better to show valor and be humane in making one's guests feel no consternation at all. The Imam also explains that when one buys a funeral shroud, there should be no haggling over the cost, for a funeral shroud should remind one of death, and a worldly matter of haggling over prices should not be involved in its obtainment. One should also not haggle over prices when buying livestock in order to give meat to the needy. The same principle applies to purchasing other goods that are intended for charity as well.

A person who doles out difficulty without cause strips away the veils of dignity; this is what the "wise guides" (the scholars) have said. It is equally regrettable when one discharges an obligation or fulfills a trust without good cheer. When paying charity, for example, one should smile and be humble, allowing the hand of the indigent to be above the giver's hand. It is a privilege to be in a position to offer charity and an honor to fulfill a divine obligation.

It is anathema to give away in charity what is shoddy and inferior. There is parsimony and miserliness in this. The Muslim tradition is to give away from what one loves; God blesses this charity and extends its goodness. "*O you who believe, spend from the good things you have earned and from what We brought out for you from the earth. And do not seek what is inferior in order to spend from it, though you yourselves would not take it unless your eyes were closed to it. And know that God is ever-rich and worthy of praise*" (QUR'AN, 2:267). And, "*You will not attain to righteousness until you spend of what you love*" (QUR'AN, 3:92).

Generosity is one of the highest virtues of Islam and one of the manifest qualities of the Prophet Muḥammad ﷺ, who was known as the most generous of people. The word for "generosity" used here is derived from the Arabic word "*karam*," which also means "nobility." In fact, one of the most excellent names of God is *al-Karīm* (the Generous). It is better to go beyond the minimum of what the sacred law demands when giving charity. This generosity is an expression of gratitude to God, who is the Provider of all wealth and provision.

The etiology of miserliness is love of the fleeting, material aspects of this world. The miser ardently clings to his wealth and hoards it. The word for "cling" in Arabic is *masak*, which is derived from another Arabic word that means "constipation." Miserly people are those who are unable to let go of something that otherwise poisons them. The Prophet ﷺ said, "God has made what is excreted from the son of Adam a metaphor for the world [*dunyā*]." When one is hungry, one seeks out food, eats, and is pleased. However, when it leaves the body, it is the most odious of things. Giving zakat is letting go of a portion of one's wealth to purify all of one's other assets and, ultimately, one's soul. It is possible that one's earnings may have some impurity in it, some doubtful source. By giving zakat, one purifies one's provision from whatever unknown impurities that may have entered.

Imam ʿAlī said, "The worst person is the miser. In this world, he is deprived of his own wealth, and in the Hereafter, he is punished." The ultimate casualty of miserliness is the miser himself. Many wealthy people in our society live impoverished lives, though they have millions in the bank. Their choice of lifestyle is not inspired by spiritual austerity. On the contrary, it causes them great discomfort to spend their money even on themselves and their families, let alone on others. The nature of the miser is that he does not benefit from his wealth in this world; and in the Hereafter he is bankrupt and debased for refusing to give to the needy. In doing so, he refuses to purify his wealth and prevents it from being a cause of light and relief in the Hereafter. The miser would argue that he hoards wealth to alleviate his fear of poverty. Remarkably, however, the miser never truly feels relieved of anxiety; a miser is constantly worried about money and devoted to servicing his worry. The Prophet ﷺ once asked some clansmen about their leader. They mentioned his name and said, "But he is a bit of a miser." The Prophet ﷺ said, "A leader should never be a miser." Then he added, "Do you know of any disease that is worse than miserliness?"

POEM VERSES 26–29

Treat this by realizing that those who achieved [affluence] did so only by exhausting themselves over long periods of time, thus finally accumulating what they sought.

Meanwhile, just as they approach the heights of [earthly] splendor, death suddenly assails them.

[Treat miserliness by also recognizing] the disdain shown to misers, and the hatred people have for them—even [hatred] amongst [misers] themselves.

With this same treatment, treat the person
whose heart's ailment is love of wealth.

Treatment

The treatment for miserliness is realizing that those who achieve wealth usually do so only after exhausting themselves over long periods of time, working for it day and night. Meanwhile, life passes on and time runs out. The culture of wanting more simply for the sake of more can occupy a person for an entire lifetime. But in the end, life is over. It terminates for the beggar and the affluent just the same, whether one is old or young, rich or poor, happy or sad.

Imam Mawlūd's counsel is to reflect long and hard on the fact that just as people climb the heights of affluence and start to achieve what they have worn themselves out for, death assails them without invitation. When death takes us and moves us on, our wealth stays behind for others to wrangle over and spend.

One must also realize the level of disdain shown to misers. Nobody likes a miser. Even misers loathe each other. Realizing the hatred people have for misers is enough to turn one away from this disease.

Wantonness

POEM VERSE 30–31

As for [the disease of] wantonness, its definition is excessive mirth, which, according to the people of knowledge, is having excessive exuberance.

Treat it with hunger and the remembrance of the Hereafter, reminding yourself that [God] says He does not love the excessively joyful—which alone is a deterrent.

Definition and Treatment

The next disease the Imam writes about is wantonness (*baṭar*), along with excessiveness, an unbridled desire to need and want more. The word *baṭar* has several meanings: "the inability to bear blessings; bewilderment; dislike of something undeserving of dislike; and reckless extravagance." Imam Mawlud says that according to the people of knowledge, it is defined as "excessive mirth and exuberance."

The Qur'an says, "*Obey God and His Messenger, and dispute not among yourselves lest you falter and your strength departs from you. And be patient, for God is with the patient. And do not be like those who leave their homes* baṭar [filled with excessive pride about their state], *showing off before people and preventing others from the way of God. And God encompasses what they do*" (QUR'AN, 8:46–47). And, "*How many cities have We destroyed that exulted in their livelihood? Here are their homes now uninhabited after them except for a few*" (QUR'AN, 28:58). The world of ancient civilizations is full of ruins of once grand structures and communities that used to be teeming with life, inhabited by people who exulted in their wealth and accomplishments. When one visits these ruins, one notices the utter silence of these towns. Each soul that lived there is now in another state, awaiting God's final judgment.

Wantonness is a disease to which the world's affluent societies are particularly vulnerable. In societies that are extremely pleased with their standard of living, their extravagance and hubris are obvious. One sign of these conditions is the ease with which people enter into debt and live contentedly with it. People are consciously living beyond their means in order to maintain the appearance of affluence. This is a product of wantonness: willingly falling headlong into debt in order to achieve a certain material standard of living.

The Imam posits that the treatment of wantonness is to intentionally experience hunger and to reflect seriously on death and the Hereafter. Experiencing hunger can be achieved through voluntary fasting (*ṣawm*) or by simply reducing what one eats. One aspect of traditional medicine related to a spiritual cosmology—whether this tradition was Greek, Chinese, or Arab—is the belief that too much food harms the spiritual heart and, in fact, could kill it. It was commonly believed that people who eat in abundance become hardhearted. Those who consume an abundance of rich foods may literally become "hardhearted" with arterial sclerosis, the hardening of the arteries. ("Sclerotic" means "hard, rigid, or stiff.") Likewise, what happens to the physical heart may parallel what occurs to the spiritual heart.

Scholars of various religions often expounded on hunger as an important sensation that feeds spiritual growth. Feeling emptiness in the stomach, they said, is excellent for the body as well as the soul. According to Imam Mālik, fasting three days out of the month is the best way to maintain a regular engagement with hunger. The fasting regimen known as the Fast of David (Dāwūd) ﷺ consists of fasting every other day, with the exception of religious holidays. Fasting Mondays and Thursdays is also an excellent regimen. Whichever pattern of fasting one chooses, it is important to maintain it, for fasting is an excellent form of worship that is beloved by God and praised by the Prophet ﷺ. It also is a protective shield against wantonness.

The second aspect to the remedy is to remember death and the Hereafter. What is meant by "remember" here is not the common function of memory, in which one merely recalls a fact without any reflection. (In fact, no spiritual remedy mentioned in this book involves a flaccid process. Each requires exertion and a true desire to achieve success in its fullest sense.) Freeing the heart of diseases such as wantonness requires remembering the Hereafter and its various states and tumultuous scenes. For example, one should reflect on the state of the grave, which will be either a parcel of Paradise or a pit of Hell. Once a person dies, his journey in the Hereafter begins. Meditation on the Hereafter requires learning more about its various stations and passages, including the Traverse (*Ṣirāṭ*), over which people must cross and behold below the awesome inferno of the Hellfire. Consistent reflection of this nature lessens the apparent value of extravagance and, in general, all the fleeting enticements this world has to offer, whether it is wealth, prestige, fame, or the like.

The Imam cites the verse, "*God does not love those who exult*" (QUR'AN, 28:76), whether it is in their wealth, status, or anything else. Images glorifying wantonness are ubiquitous in our times. Even as one drives, he or she is accosted by billboard advertisements that show the faces of wantonness: people in ecstatic postures with exaggerated smiles and gaping mouths, showing off their supreme happiness because they own a particular type of car or smoke a certain brand of cigarettes or guzzle a special brand of beer—alcohol that destroys lives and minds. According to advertising theory, when people are constantly exposed to such images, they not only incline toward the product but desire the culture associated with it. Advertisers sell a lifestyle that glorifies wantonness and subtly dissuades reflection. All those smiling people on billboards and all those who aim their glances toward them will inevitably die someday and stand before their Maker. This is the ultimate destiny of all human beings. It is this realization that is the slayer of wantonness.

Hatred

POEM VERSES 32–33

Another disease is hatred for other than the sake of [God,] the Exalted. Its cure is to pray for the one despised.

This is with the understanding that you have not done wrong if you are repulsed by the hatred you harbor and do not act in accordance with it [to harm the person].

Definition and Treatment

The next disease is hatred (*bughḍ*). In itself, hatred is not necessarily negative. It is commendable to hate corruption, evil, disbelief, murder, lewdness, and anything else that God has exposed as despicable. The Prophet ﷺ never disliked the essence of anything, but only what something manifested.

Hatred or strong dislike of a person for no legitimate reason is the disease of *bughḍ*. The Prophet ﷺ once said to his Companions, "Do you want to see a man of Paradise?" A man then passed by, and the Prophet ﷺ said, "That man is of the people of Paradise." One of Companion of the Prophet ﷺ wanted to find out what it was about this man that earned him such a commendation from the Messenger of God ﷺ, so he decided to spend some time with this man and observe him closely. He noticed that this man did not perform the night prayer vigil (*tahajjud*) or do anything extraordinary. He appeared to be an average man of Medina. The Companion finally told the man what the Prophet ﷺ had said about him and asked if he did anything special. The man replied, "The only thing that I can think of, other than what everybody else does, is that I make sure that I never sleep with any rancor in my heart towards another." That was his secret.

The cure for hatred is straightforward. One should pray for the person toward whom he feels hatred, making specific supplications that mention this person by name, asking God to give this person good things in this life and the next. When one does this with sincerity, hearts mend. If one truly wants to purify his or her heart and root out disease, there must be total sincerity in carrying out the treatments and conviction that these cures are effective.

Arguably, the disease of hatred is one of the most devastating forces in the world. But the force that is infinitely more powerful is love. Love is an attribute of God; hate is not. A name of God mentioned in the Qur'an is *al-Wadūd*, the Loving One. Hate is the absence of love, and only through love can hatred be removed from the heart. In a beautiful hadith, the Prophet ﷺ said, "None of you has achieved faith until he loves for his brother what he loves for himself." The thirteenth century scholar Imam al-Nawawī comments on this hadith:

> When the Prophet ﷺ says "brother," we should interpret this as universal brotherhood, which includes Muslims and non-Muslims. For one should desire for his brother non-Muslim that he enter into the state of submission with his Lord [Islam]. And for his brother Muslim, he should love for him the continuation of guidance and that he remain in submission. Because of this, it is considered highly recommended and divinely rewarding to pray for a non-Muslim's guidance. The word "love" here refers to a desire for good and for benefit to come to others. This love is celestial or spiritual love and not earthly or human love, for human nature causes people to desire harm to befall their enemies and to discriminate against those who are unlike them [in creed, color, or character]. However, men must oppose their nature, pray for their brothers, and desire for others what they desire for themselves. Moreover, whenever a man does not desire good for his brother, envy is the root cause. Envy is a rejection of God's apportionment in the world. Thus, one is opposing how God meted out sustenance in accord with His wisdom. Therefore, one must oppose his own ego's desires and seek treatment for this disease with the healing force of acceptance of the divine decree and prayer on behalf of one's enemies in a way that suppresses the ego [*nafs*].

Iniquity

POEM VERSES 34–42

[The disease of] iniquity, according to the book, Opening of the Truth, is defined as harming a fellow creature without right.

Its cause is the powerfully intoxicating wine, "love of [worldly] position." So remember—if you wish to turn [this intoxicant] into useful vinegar—

How many a leader achieved his heart's desire of rank and position, yet in the end, the devotee and his object of devotion were leveled to equal planes [by death].

Keep in mind that this desire is about turning away from your Master towards His impoverished and miserly servants.

Concern with the affections of others is exhausting, and though you may please some, others will flee from you, filled with anger.

Yet what is prohibited regarding the pleasure of others is what is procured by way of trickery, ostentatious display of religiosity, or hypocritical affectation.

[Know also] that the seeker of their pleasure cannot expect the pleasure of [God,] the Fashioner of creation, the Mighty, the Capable.

As for the one whose heart is encrusted with the love of this world, his only cure is having certainty [of his mortality].

Thus, if he keeps death constantly before his eyes, this acts as a cleanser for the soiled matter encrusting his heart.

Definition and Treatment

Iniquity is defined, according to Shaykh Muḥammad, the author of the book, *The Opening of the Truth*, as harming anything in creation without just cause. The word is a translation of *baghī*, which is derived from the Arabic word that denotes "desire." In this context, the problem is desiring something to the point of transgressing the rights of others to attain it. The iniquity and injustice that people aim at others ultimately work against themselves: "*O you people, surely your iniquity is but against your selves*" (QUR'AN, 10:23). Imam Mawlūd describes the cause of iniquity using the metaphor of a powerfully intoxicating wine, called *qarqaf*, which makes one shudder when swallowed. This metaphorical wine is "love of position," which is a major motivation that impels some people to wrong others. Even petty office managers oppress their subordinates for the purpose of marking their territory and securing their positions. Tyrants on corporate boards pull off power plays to acquire more authority or remove those whom they perceive to be potential challenges to their authority or position.

The Imam states that the desire for temporal power is a move away from God—besides whom there is no power or might—and a move toward His creation, that is, people who are by comparison impoverished. Those desiring temporal power protect whatever illusory possessions and authority they have like misers.

Vain pursuits wear out the soul. A person who endeavors to please people and gain their love, admiration, or approval will exhaust himself. In the end, his pursuit may leave some people pleased and happy, but others displeased and resentful. It is said that if one honors a noble man, he reciprocates honorably, but if one honors a vile person, he responds with anger and resentment. The poet, al-Mutanabbī, said, "Whenever you honor the honorable, you possess them. Whenever you honor the ignoble, they rebel."

It is prohibited to seek the pleasure of others through trickery, ostentatious religiosity, or hypocritical flattery. One should not expect the pleasure of God when pursuing the pleasure of His creatures. Scholars have pointed out that seeking the pleasure of God actually makes a person pleasing to good people. One should not be concerned with the commendation of the corrupt, the miserly, power-hungry, and their like. It is a tremendous waste of time seeking those whose commendations are of no real value. Honor and rank are forever linked with the status one has with God. The great Muslim scholar, Ibn ʿAṭā'allāh (d. 709/1309), said, "If you desire immortal glory, seek glory in the Immortal."

The Imam uses the word *ummih*, which, in this context, means "world," though its dominant meaning is "mother" (the connection between the two definitions is that we are made from the material of this world). However, love of this ephemeral world encrusts the heart, as this type of love involves dedication to the material world at the expense of spiritual ascendancy. Love like this keeps a person's eyes toward the earth—figuratively speaking—and makes one heedless of the ultimate return to God.

The cure for this is having certainty in the ultimate destiny of humanity. Envisioning standing in the Hereafter for judgment has the power to expose the utter waste of irrelevant pursuits. The Prophet ﷺ said, "Remember often the destroyer of pleasure," that is, death. Remembering death is a spiritual practice that cleanses the heart of frivolousness. The Prophet ﷺ once passed by a group of Muslims who were laughing heartily, and he said to them, "Mix in your gatherings the remembrance of death." This is not a prohibition against laughter but a reminder that prolonged amusement has the capacity to anesthetize the soul. Someone once asked ʿĀ'ishah رضي الله عنها, the Prophet's wife, about the most wondrous aspect she observed of the Prophet ﷺ. She said, "Everything about him was wondrous. But I will say this: when the veiling of the night came, and when every lover went to his lover, he went to be with God." The Prophet ﷺ stood at night in prayer, remembering his Lord until his ankles swelled up and his tears dripped from his beard. The Prophet ﷺ said, "Death is closer to any of you than the strap on his sandals." Somewhere on earth there is a door reserved for each soul, and one day each of us will walk through that door never to return to this life again. Where that door is and when we will walk through it are unknowns that we must live with and prepare for.

Upon death, suddenly all of this—this whole world and all of its charms and occupations—will become as if it were all a dream: "*And you will think that you tarried [on earth] only for a short while*" (QUR'AN, 17:52). Even those who are spiritually blind will see in the new order of existence the ultimate truth about God and our purpose as His creation. And when we climb out of our graves for the mighty Gathering in the Hereafter, it will seem to us that we had stayed in our graves for only a day or part of a day, as the Qur'an states (10:45). When one is confronted with eternity and its ironclad reality, this world will seem like the most ephemeral of existences. This once overwhelmingly alluring life will be of no value to anyone.

Even the world's most powerful leaders, after finally achieving what they so badly coveted, taste death. All their power abruptly vanishes at death's door, the great leveler. Their minions die just the same, those who did whatever they could to move closer to people of authority. When one examines the conduct of the Companions, it is clear that they sought to be nearer to the Prophet ﷺ to learn more about their obligations and what would draw them closer to God. They did not desire illusory power. The believers around the Prophet ﷺ saw first hand that God chose him ﷺ to be the conveyor and exemplar of the final message sent to humanity. Learning at the hand of the Prophet ﷺ provides meanings and benefits that extend beyond this life. Attaining nearness to God does not involve wronging others. On the contrary, access to the source of all power requires a character that is selfless, compassionate, and sensitive to the rights of others.

It serves the soul to be actively aware that the door to death awaits each human being and that it can open at any time. For this reason, the Imam says that we must keep the spectacle of death before our eyes and realize its proximity.

Love of the World

POEM VERSES 43–53

Realize also that blameworthy love of this world is what is solely for the benefit of the self. It does not include desiring it so that others are not burdened

by your needs, and so that you are secure from dependence upon other people. Nor does it include desiring it as provision for the next world.

Indeed, love of this world falls under [the five categories of] legal rulings, such that its [acceptability or detriment] is based on what it helps one to achieve. If the love of something of this world is for the purpose of helping one achieve something prohibited, then it is also prohibited.

As such, censuring the world is only for those things that do not advance [one's] salvation. Thus, for these reasons, censuring is restricted to its ardent love. Indeed, the best of creation [the Prophet ﷺ] prohibited cursing the world.

Things are praised or censured only by virtue of what results from them, like healing or disease. Therefore, what is obtained for [one's] physical necessities, by means of wealth or worldly position, is beneficial.

Still, some scholars scorn the accumulation of great wealth, fearing [the risk] of transgressing the bounds of permissibility.

One who earns wealth for the purpose of vainglorious competition is reckoned as among those who perpetrate enormities.

Love of praise for what one has not accomplished is caused by desiring other than [God,] the Exalted.

Definition and Treatment

An Islamic tradition attributed to Jesus ﷺ states, "The world is a bridge; so pass over it to the next world, but do not try to build on it." Love of this world is considered blameworthy, though this does not include wanting things of this world in order to be free from burdening others with one's needs, nor does it include desiring provision from the world for the purpose of attaining the best of the Hereafter.

The five categories of classical legal rulings determine how love of something worldly is viewed. Depending on the intentions of the person, the love of this world can either be obligatory (*wājib*), recommended (*mandūb*), permissible (*mubāḥ*), reprehensible (*makrūh*), or forbidden (*ḥarām*). For example, we should love aspects of this world that helps us achieve felicity in the Hereafter, such as the Qur'an, the Ka'ba, the Prophet ﷺ, our parents, godly people, books of knowledge, children, and others who help us in our religious affairs. As for wealth, we should love helping the needy with it.

The Prophet ﷺ prohibited vilification of the world. He said, "Do not curse the world, for God created the world, and the world is a means to reaching [knowledge of] God." The Qur'an states, "*And He has subjugated for you what is in the heavens and what is on earth, all of it from Him. Indeed, therein are sure signs for a people who reflect*" (QUR'AN, 45:13). The world is the greatest sign of God, as is the cosmos. We do not accept the doctrine of condemning the world, which is found in some religious traditions. We say that He created everything in the world and has subjugated its resources for our just and conscientious use. What is censured is loving those things that are sinful or that lead to sinful matters and loving the ephemeral aspects of the world to the point that it suppresses one's spiritual yearning.

The Imam says that love of the world is praised or blamed based on what good or harm it brings to a person. If it leads to a diseased heart—such as greediness and arrogance—then it is blameworthy. If it leads to spiritual elevation and healing of the heart, then it is praiseworthy. Anything that is obtained from the necessities of living on earth—food, housing, shelter, and the like—is beneficial and is not considered "worldly" per se. Attaining wealth and position for the benefit of the needy is not considered blameworthy. What scholars traditionally have warned against, with regard to attaining wealth, is the danger of eventual transgression. The more wealth one acquires, the higher the probability that one will become preoccupied with other than God. Also, vying for wealth can become an addiction and lead to ostentation, which is considered a disease of the heart.

Love of praise is another disease, particularly the love of praise for something one has not done. This is caused by desiring something from other than God. People naturally love praise, but it should be for something one has actually done. Furthermore, the cause of praise should be something that is praiseworthy in the sight of God. It is not necessarily wrong to want people to appreciate what one has done. When the Prophet ﷺ learned of the good that someone had done, he would say, "May God reward you with goodness." One must make the distinction between flattery and appreciation. The Prophet ﷺ said, "Throw dirt in the faces of flatterers," those who pour accolades upon others, worthy or not, like poets who compose appallingly obsequious poetry praising a tyrant. But praising or thanking someone for doing good is expressing gratitude. The Prophet ﷺ said, "Whoever is not thankful to people will not be thankful to God." Flatter, on the other hand, is being disingenuous with praise. People often praise others because they want something from them. What is particularly blameworthy is when people enjoy receiving praise for something they have not done. "*Do not think that those who rejoice in what they have done and who love to be praised for what they have not done—do not think that they will escape punishment. Theirs shall be a painful chastisement*" (QUR'AN, 3:188). For example, in academia, some professors receive tribute for work their students actually did. In the corporate culture, it is not unheard of for managers to be credited for the accomplishment of a team of people, to whom the managers sometimes attribute nothing.

Envy

POEM VERSES 54–58

If you were to describe your desire that someone lose his blessing as "envy," then your description will be accurate.

In other words, if you yourself were able, through some ruse, to eliminate [someone's blessing], you would utilize that ruse to do so.

But if the fear of [God], the Eternally Besought, prevents you from doing so, then you are not an envious person.

This is what the Proof of Islam [Imam al-Ghazālī] expected with hope from the bounty of the Possessor of Majesty and Generosity.

He said that whoever despises envy such that he loathes it in himself is safeguarded from fulfilling what it customarily necessitates.

Definition

Envy (*ḥasad*) is a severe disease of the heart that some scholars hold to be the root of all diseases, while others opine that the parent disease goes back to covetousness (*ṭamaʿ*).

Regardless of where envy ranks in the hierarchy of diseases, most scholars agree that it is the first manifestation of wrongdoing and the first cause of disobedience against God. It occurred when Satan (Iblīs) refused to obey God when commanded to bow down before the new creation, Adam, the first human being. Nothing prevented Iblīs from bowing down except his envy of Adam, for God chose Adam to be His vicegerent on earth instead of him. Iblīs arrogantly objected to the command that he show Adam any honor, for Iblīs saw himself, a creation from fire, superior to Adam, created merely from clay. When confronted with his disobedience, Satan did not seek forgiveness from God. Enviers develop a mindset that makes it impossible for them to admit they are wrong. To manifest envy is to manifest one of the characteristics of the most wretched creature, Satan.

In Arabic, *ḥasūd* (or *ḥāsid*) is one who carries and emanates this envy, and the object of one's envy is called *maḥsūd*. The Qur'an teaches us to seek refuge in God from "*the evil of the envier* [ḥāsid] *when he envies*" (QUR'AN, 113:5). The Prophet ﷺ said that envy consumes good deeds the way fire devours dry wood. The Prophet ﷺ also said, "Every possessor of any blessing is envied." Someone of means will have someone who envies him for what he possesses. Even a street sweeper may be envied. If he owns a donkey to pull his cart and another street sweeper has no donkey and has to pull his cart, this can be a cause for envy.

While it is believed that envy can bring about harm to the one envied, ultimately it is the envier who is harmed the most. The evil eye is generally related to envy, though not necessarily so. Some people simply have "the eye," some type of psychic power that does not necessitate envy. Every culture has a concept of the evil eye. In some cultures, parents used to pierce the ears of their firstborn males and dress them as little girls for the first five years, since firstborn males were so coveted. Many Chinese conduct rituals to prevent the evil eye from afflicting their homes by placing mirrors on walls to reflect evil looks. (The word "invidious" means, "envy," and it originally meant to look at something with a malevolent or evil eye.)

The Prophet ﷺ said, "The evil eye is true." The evil eye is not superstition. The Prophet ﷺ worked to eradicate superstition from the minds of people. For example, the Arabs believed that when the moon eclipsed it meant that a great person died. When a lunar eclipse occurred on the day the Prophet's infant son, Ibrāhīm, died, many of the Arabs were impressed by this phenomenon. While a charlatan would have seized the moment to take advantage of such an event, the Prophet ﷺ announced to the people, "The moon is a sign of God; the sun is a sign of God. They do not eclipse for anyone."

Imam Mawlūd explains that envy is exhibited when one desires that another person lose a blessing he or she has. This loss could be anything big or small—a house, a car, a job, etc. For example, an envious person may become resentful that a coworker was promoted, to the point that he wishes that the person lose the position. A woman may envy another woman because of her husband such that she hopes that a marital crisis separate the couple. A man may grow envious over another man's wife. There are endless variations of envy, but a common thread is the desire that someone lose a blessing. In essence, envy arises over what one perceives to be a blessing in someone else's possession.

A blessing (*niʿmah*) is something that God bestows. One of God's names is *al-Munʿim*, the Bestower of Blessing. Envy, then, is to desire that a person lose whatever blessing God has given him or her. It is tantamount to saying that God should not have given this person a blessing or, worse yet, that He was wrong to do so "because I deserve it more." As the Imam says, it may reach the point that an envier would himself remove the blessing if he were able to do so through some kind of ruse. However, what is perceived as a blessing could be based on a completely false notion, as one may desire something that in reality is nothing but trouble and difficulty. Conversely, there could be a blessing hidden in something difficult.

There is a well-known story about al-Aṣmaʿī, the famous Arab philologist and compiler of poetry, when he once came upon a Bedouin and was invited to enter his tent. In Bedouin culture, the women serve guests in the presence of their husbands. This Bedouin had a very beautiful wife, though he himself was quite unattractive. When the men went out to prepare a lamb for a meal, the guest couldn't resist saying to this woman, "How did such a beautiful woman like you marry such an ugly man like that?" The woman said, "Fear God! Perhaps he had done good works accepted by his Lord, and I am his reward." God is all-wise in what He gives to people. If one questions the blessing a person has received, then he or she is actually questioning the Giver. This makes envy reprehensible and forbidden.

POEM VERSES 59–62

As for the cure, it is to act contrary to [one's] caprice.

For example, being beneficent to a person when it seems appealing to harm him, or praising him when you desire to find fault in him.

Also [the cure is in] knowing that envy only harms the envier; it causes him to be grievously preoccupied [with his object of envy] today, and tomorrow he is thereby punished.

Moreover, [envy] never benefits [the envier], nor does it remove from the one envied the blessing he has been given.

Treatment

Imam Mawlūd prescribes two cures for envy. The first is to consciously act in opposition to one's caprice. The Arabic term here for caprice (*hawā*) is derived from the Arabic word that means, "to fall." It is also related to the Arabic word for "wind." One's passion is like the wind, in that it comes, stirs up emotion, and then dies down. One cannot really see it, only its effect.

More often than not, following one's whims takes a person away from the truth. The history of humanity is replete with false notions that have come and gone. The truth, however, is something that is fixed and that can be recognized as such, if one is truly objective. As for caprice, it has no foundation. For this reason, Imam Mawlūd says one must resist his caprice. The Qur'an repeatedly warns against following one's caprice. It speaks of bygone communities who grew arrogant when God's messengers came to them with admonitions and teachings that did not agree with their souls' caprice. So they rejected the message and even killed the messengers (QUR'AN, 5:70). Also, God praises those who resist the caprices of their souls and promises them Paradise (QUR'AN, 79:40). One of the names of Hell mentioned in the Qur'an is *hāwiyah* (QUR'AN, 101:9), which is derived from the same root as *hawā*. Perhaps the connection is that a person enslaved to his whims descends into the depths of depravity in this life, and, as a consequence, he faces perdition in the Hereafter. As a remedy to the type of envy that prods one to bring about harm to another person, Imam Mawlūd suggests that one contradict his temptation, that is, do something that will benefit the person who is envied. For example, give that person a gift or do a favor. This defies the commands of one's whims, gains the pleasure of God, and protects against envy. The Imam suggests also that one may praise the person toward whom one feels the urge to slander. There is no hypocrisy in this recommendation. The purpose is to starve envy of the negative thoughts it requires to thrive. Being beneficent to a person against whom one feels envy often makes that person incline towards the envier. In general, good people are inclined to love those who show them good.

Another treatment is to know with certainty that holding envy against another person brings harm to oneself. Human nature's most primordial instinct is to avoid harm. It is easier for a person to repel negative feelings when he or she realizes these feelings hurt the soul. For example, if a disgruntled worker becomes anxious and angry because he is passed over for a promotion, his anxiety and anger harm his soul, mind, and body, and yield nothing for his future. In complaining at length and becoming obsessed with the object of his envy, the person to whom the promotion was granted, he permits the disease to fester in his heart and cause him grief. These cascading feelings will neither help him ascend in his profession nor alter the past. It is an entirely demoralizing exercise that can magnify the original injury he felt. Envy, in fact, can actually damage one's sanity. Resentment may prevent one from accomplishing significant achievements. A person who shuns envy, even when others around him seem to be passing him by, is motivated to excel, unimpeded by depression and resentment.

Unfortunately, the Muslim world is now filled with envy. For example, when many Muslims look at Americans and Europeans, they hurl criticisms, applying all kinds of rhetoric. Ostensibly, one hears moral outrage. However, the root of much of this rhetoric is envy:

"They have worldly possessions, and we do not" is what often comes across. Similarly, when many less fortunate Muslims glance toward the Gulf nations that have great stores of oil, they cannot resist passing judgment about how the Gulf Arabs squander "Muslim money." This type of dialogue stems from envy. The issue is comparing what one has with what another has, and that only fuels envy and brings about no positive impact. This does not mean that one should not criticize; however, criticism should be done with the purpose of being constructive and not destructive.

The Communist Revolution was largely a manifestation of envy. The writings of Karl Marx indicate that he was filled with resentment. Much of his theory is founded on observing the wealthy and desiring that they lose what they have. This is not to suggest that when the wealthy are unjust to the poor and to the working class they should not be censured, but from the point of view of sacred law, both the affluent and the needy have their respective obligations. An obligation of the poor is not to envy the rich and harbor resentment toward them; and the rich are obligated to not belittle the indigent, grow arrogant, hoard wealth, or work to keep others in need.

The Imam says that one way to uproot envy is to realize with solemn reflection that envy can never benefit its agent. One should also realize that what people attain in terms of material wealth or prestige is from God. He is all-knowing and all-wise; He knows best how to distribute His blessings and to whom, while we do not possess such knowledge.

The basis of the remedy for envy is *taqwā*, which is having a sense of awe of God, an active awareness of Him as the ultimate power over all creation. This defuses false notions of misappropriated blessings. A hadith states, "If you have envy, do not wrong [others]." If one does not work to remove another person's blessings, then his or her envy is in check and is not the kind that necessarily devours one's goods deeds. Envy that devours righteous deeds is envy that impels someone to wrong others. Imam al-Ghazālī makes a distinction between various strains of envy. He states that if one hates envy and is ashamed that he or she harbors it, the person is not essentially an envious person. It is important to be aware of the feelings that reside in one's heart. This self-awareness is essential for the purpose of purification.

POEM VERSES 63–66

Its etiology includes animosity, vying for the love of others,
arrogance, poor self-worth, vanity,

Love of leadership, and avaricious cupidity [for things].
These [seven] causes engender envy.

As for a blessing that a disbeliever or corrupt Muslim
has that enables one to harm others or show aggression

Because of it, then the "malady of second wives"
is in such instances permissible.

Etiology

The Imam now delves into the etiology of the disease, for without discovering the causes of envy, it would be difficult to excise it. The first cause he mentions is enmity (*ʿadāwah*). Harboring feelings of animosity toward another makes one highly susceptible to developing envy. Another cause of envy is vying for another's affection or love, which can become vicious; and its effect can linger in a person for a very long time, which is often the case when siblings compete for parental love. (On this topic, one may read Frank J. Sulloway's *Born to Rebel*, a book with a complex statistical study about birth order and how children are affected by it—how competition for parental love and attention informs a child's personality.)

The Imam next mentions arrogance (*takabbur*), a major cause of envy. An arrogant man who sees someone advancing ahead of him will feel that this person is not worthy of such advancement. The pre-Islamic Arabs exhibited this when the Prophet ﷺ preached. The disbelievers among the Quraysh, like Abū Jahl, Umayyah ibn Khalaf, and al-Walīd ibn al-Mughīrah, displayed their arrogance by rejecting that Muḥammad ﷺ, this man among them, their own kin, received revelation from God. The Qur'an exposes their feelings, informing us that each of them secretly wished to receive a revelation from Heaven the way the Prophet ﷺ did (QUR'AN, 74:52). This was flagrant envy aimed at the Prophet ﷺ. When people regard each other as equal, arrogance does not foster. However, when someone is suddenly elevated in rank, the dynamics change. Pharaoh grew arrogant and envious when Prophet Moses ﷺ came to him with God's message. Part of Pharaoh's problem was seeing that a prophet was chosen from among people whom he had enslaved and whom he regarded as lower than the Egyptians.

Imam Mawlūd mentions as another cause for envy low self-esteem (*ta*ʿ*azzuz*), the feeling that one's worth is compromised by the fact that another person has gained more. This also was a pathology found in the days of the Prophet ﷺ, when the disbelievers of Quraysh protested aloud, "*If only this Qur'an had been sent down to a great man of either of the two cities!*" (QUR'AN, 43:31). In other words, they were so entrenched in their mode of tribalism that they could not accept the fact that Muḥammad ﷺ was a true prophet because he was not one of the elite of "the two cities," that is, Mecca and Ta'if. In their view, Muḥammad ﷺ was too ordinary for them, too much like them, to have been chosen for such a lofty station. They felt, "How can he be a prophet, while he is like us, and we are not prophets?"

Love of leadership is another major cause of envy. People in leadership positions often resent others achieving something significant, fearing a change in the equilibrium of power. The envious leader desires that others are deprived of accomplishment and authority. This is akin to covetousness, which the Imam also mentions in the same line. There is, though, a distinction between covetousness and love of leadership. The latter afflicts those who have position already, while covetousness relates to those who do not have it but desire it avariciously. This type of covetousness, called *shuḥḥ* in Arabic, is a desire to have what is in possession of another person.

God says, "*Whoever is safe from the covetousness of his own soul, he is truly successful*" (QUR'AN, 59:9).

According to Imam al-Ghazālī, because these diseases are common to human nature, the objective should be to transform them into something beneficial, to transform a disability into an advantage, which is what successful people tend to do. The Prophet ﷺ said, "There is no [acceptable] envy except of two people." One of them is a person who has been given wealth and spends it toward good causes. Envying such a person is permissible because one's desire is to have wealth in order to do the righteous deed of giving to the needy. One may envy such a person, desiring to be able to do the same good as well, but not in the sense of hoping that he loses his wealth. The other person is one who has been given wisdom and teaches it to people. A person may envy the wise because he or she wishes to be imbued with some of that wisdom as well in order to teach others. Hence, if one has envy, one should let it not be of fleeting things, like worldly assets that are usually hoarded and displayed for show. One should instead desire what will serve one's Hereafter. This is how to convert negative feelings into positive ones.

Blameworthy Modesty

POEM VERSES 67–72

As for blameworthy modesty, it is that which prevents one from denouncing the condemnable or from asking a question concerning

A matter relating to religion and the like. For this reason, it is considered a harmful quality.

As for noble modesty, [it is] such as the Chosen One's behavior the night he married Zaynab,

When he fed his company to their full from his wedding feast, and they all left except for three.

They lingered, yet he did not request that they leave. Such modesty is a most excellent virtue.

Had modesty been a person, it would have been a righteous one and would do nothing but good in whatever it did.

Definition

In general, modesty is something praised in Islam and is considered virtuous. Modesty becomes blameworthy if it prevents one from denouncing what clearly should be denounced, such as tyranny or corruption. This form of modesty results in meekness at a time when one needs to be forthright and courageous. Something condemnable (*munkar*) is condemnable regardless of the status of the person who is engaged in it—whether he or she is a close relative or a person of status, wealth, or authority.

There must be agreement, however, among scholars on what is condemnable. One cannot, for example, declare decisively that something is considered condemnable if there is a difference of opinion on it among the scholars. Scholars knowledgeable of the plentitude of juristic differences rarely condemn others. They refrain from such condemnation not because of modesty but because of their extensive knowledge and scholarly insight. Unfortunately, many people today are swift to condemn, which creates another disease: self-righteousness.

Blameworthy modesty results in timid failure to denounce what unequivocally deserves denouncement or to ask about important matters from those who are knowledgeable. The Prophet's wife ʿĀ'ishah once said, "The best women were the women of the Anṣār because modesty did not prevent them from learning the religion." A woman once came to the Prophet ﷺ asking a specific question about menstruation. The Prophet ﷺ answered her, but the woman persisted in asking for more detail. The Prophet ﷺ then asked ʿĀ'ishah to show the woman what he meant, for it was awkward for him. Some women even sent the cloth used for their menstrual protection to seek out with certainty what constitutes the beginning and the end of the menses, which determines whether or not certain rites of worship may be resumed. Most women would not feel comfortable with that, but the modesty of these women did not prevent them from seeking out knowledge about their religious affairs.

The Imam speaks next of virtuous modesty which is rooted in generosity and kindness; this is an acceptable kind of modesty. He gives the example of the behavior of the Prophet ﷺ when he married Zaynab. The Prophet ﷺ invited people for a wedding ceremony and meal. The guests came but lingered in his presence much longer than necessary. In fact, three of them remained late into the evening. The Prophet ﷺ, in his generosity, stayed with them and patiently waited for his guests to complete their visit. The guests, however, tarried with the Prophet ﷺ because they loved his company. At one point, the Prophet ﷺ stood up, left the room, and then came back, hinting as gently as possible that they should depart. But they sill lingered. He did this again, and then a verse was revealed with regard to the etiquette of being in another's home—an admonition that the Prophet ﷺ himself was too shy and generous to deliver: "*[Believers], when you are invited, then enter. And when you have completed the meal, disperse, and do not linger on for conversation. This used to hurt the Prophet, but he shied away from [telling] you. But God is not shy of the truth*" (QUR'AN, 33:53). This verse applies, in particular, to visiting people whose obligations and time constraints are greater than others, such as statesmen and scholars. They may also feel shy about cutting visits short when they are the hosts.

The Prophet ﷺ was too modest to tell his guests that it was time to leave. It was out of his generosity and benevolence that he did not address his guests this way. Of course, some people would feel no consternation at all in asking their guests to leave, and they would do so in unambiguous terms. Imagine then how pure and wonderful was the Prophet ﷺ, the final Messenger sent to humanity, a man bestowed with great authority from God Himself, yet he was still too shy to request his loitering guests to leave on his wedding night.

The Imam concludes this section saying that had modesty been a man, he would have been a righteous man whose actions would always be virtuous.

Fantasizing

POEM VERSES 73–74

The heart's engagement in matters that do not concern it is only forbidden when it pertains to the prohibited,

Such as fantasizing about the beautiful qualities of a woman or [dwelling] on the faults of Muslims, even in their absence.

Discussion

The next disease is when one's heart is engaged in matters that are of no concern to him. For example, reflecting on things that are prohibited, such as lustful fantasizing about the beauty of a person one is not married to. In essence, if an action is forbidden, reflecting on that action is also forbidden.

Thinking about the weaknesses or faults of others is forbidden, whether they are present or not. The Prophet ﷺ said, "There is a tree in Paradise reserved for one whose own faults preoccupied him from considering the faults of others." Spending time thinking or talking about other people's faults is foolish. Time is short and is better invested in recognizing one's own shortcomings and then working consistently to eradicate them.

It is also prohibited, according to scholars, to reflect on the nature of God's essence. This does not mean that one should not reflect on His attributes revealed in the Qur'an. Rather, trying to conceive of the very essence of God is beyond our capability, and so our conclusions will always be wrong. Being wrong about something like this is not inconsequential. Many religious communities before Islam as well as after indulged in this activity and have come up with terribly erroneous theologies regarding God. For this reason, we are told to stay away from that kind of internal or external dialogue and reflect instead on what God has revealed about Himself and His awesome majesty, knowledge, and power. That kind of reflection deepens one's love of Him and one's desire to follow His commandments and thus prepare for the Hereafter, a momentous time when the veils will be removed from our eyes and when our understanding of God will reach beyond what is possible in this world.

Fear of Poverty

POEM VERSES 75–77

Fear of poverty originates in having a bad opinion of [God,] the Exalted, and its cure is in having a good opinion

And knowing that what God possesses is never diminished in the least [by His expenditure from it] and that what has been apportioned to you will reach you inevitably.

One who uses his religion as a means of benefiting his worldly condition is a sycophantic hypocrite in his transaction, and he ultimately shall be the one defrauded.

Discussion

The next spiritual disease Imam Mawlūd discusses is fear of poverty. Scholars have said that nurturing this fear is tantamount to harboring a negative opinion about God, the Exalted, who has revealed, "*Satan threatens you with poverty, and he commands you to immorality. But God promises you His forgiveness and bounty*" (QUR'AN, 2:268). One of Satan's tactics is to keep people so occupied with fear of losing their wealth that this culminates in them desperately clinging to their money and depriving the needy—and themselves—of the goodness of giving for the sake of God. A person under the spell of irrational fear is more vulnerable to transgressing laws, even to the point of indulging in lewdness, for the purpose of gaining profit and wealth.

God is the Provider and source of all wealth and comfort. He has promised that those who believe in Him and expend on behalf of the indigent shall receive a far more valuable return than the measure of what they spend. If one is to have fear, it should be of God, who has revealed, "*And whoever fears God, He will make for him a way out. And He will provide for him in a way he never expected. And whoever trusts in God, He is sufficient for him*" (QUR'AN, 65:2–3).

The stipulations in receiving this provision are that one have true *taqwā* (God consciousness) and nurture it so that it permits one to walk the earth with dignity.

Fear of poverty is an instrument of deception and a common cause of misguidance. The American humorist, Mark Twain, once remarked, "I've had thousands of problems in my life. Most of which never actually happened." A person can grieve over a plethora of concerns and problems that he or she may never have to face. These phantom concerns can be crippling. Wealthy people cannot be at peace if constantly worried about their estate and its potential loss. Many wealthy people enjoy no peace of mind, and their lives are rife with conflict, contention, and treachery. A hadith states, "Anxiety is half of aging." Another hadith states, "Righteousness will lengthen your life." One interpretation of this hadith is that people who are righteous do not suffer anxiety that tears down the body and mind. They are content to do good deeds, and they trust in God. It is usually the irreligious who are in a state of turmoil, with hearts not at ease.

Imam Mawlūd ties "fear of poverty" with a kindred illness whose carrier is called *mudāhin* in Arabic; it is a person who uses his religion as a means of buttressing his worldly condition. He is a "sycophantic hypocrite in his transaction," which culminates in his cheating himself in the most debased way. He compromises his religion in order to achieve worldly gain, often out of fear of poverty or sheer greediness.

In the Qur'an, God exposes the disbelievers among the Quraysh who tried to make deals and compromises with the Prophet ﷺ in an attempt to make his religion a means to tend to their worldly affairs. God says about them, "*They would love that you [O Muḥammad] compromise so that they may compromise*" (QUR'AN, 68:9). They desired that the Prophet ﷺ praise their gods and their rituals, even though he did not believe in them, and they, in turn, would not oppress the Prophet ﷺ and the Muslims. With this deal, the Meccans could keep their grip on the city and the trade caravans that come to it.

The great historian, Ibn Khaldūn, quoted a poet's observation of the Muslim societies he came across: "We mend our livelihood with the cloth of our religion. In the end, nothing of the religion remains, and our worldly condition goes unmended." God will never set aright one's worldly affairs when he or she destroys religion.

Mudāhana is from the root word *duhun*, which means, "to cover something up with paint or cosmetics." Shaykh Muḥammad al-Yadālī says that *mudāhana* is when a man "gives up his religion in order to secure his wealth or his blood, sitting with the people of disobedience, keeping their company, praising their actions, and displaying pleasure at their condition without condemnation." In our modern context, *mudāhana* may be applied to a conspiracy of silence when it comes to other people's transgressions and blatant deviations. It is turning one's eyes away from those who commit abominations for some worldly gain.

Treatment

The cure for fear of poverty is to have a good opinion of God, says the Imam. God states, "*I do not desire from [people] any provision, nor do I desire that they feed Me*" (QUR'AN, 51:57). People who harbor good thoughts about their Provider deflect insidious whisperings about Him and the subtle provocations that create irrational fear. His dominion is never diminished in the least when He gives to His creation all that they need. And if someone else is given more, one should not harbor bad thoughts toward that person. Wholesome thoughts about God express themselves in one's contentment with what he or she has and not in stretching one's eyes toward the assets of others. The Prophet ﷺ said, "Contentment is a treasure that is never exhausted."

Ostentation

POEM VERSES 78–86

Its root cause is covetousness and [doing good works for the sake of] showing off. The cure [for covetousness] is also my cure for the next disease [ostentation].

So roll up your sleeves if you want to set out and cure what is at the root of all of these diseases and what exacerbates them.

I mean that showing off is one of the calamities of the heart, [whose definition is] to perform an act of devotion for other than the Creator's sake.

Rather, it is for the purpose of seeking some worldly benefit or praise from His creation, or to protect oneself from the opposite, [that is, loss of wealth or dispraise].

The worst form is that which results in a sinful deed, such as pretentious display of virtue,

so as to be entrusted with the wealth of an orphan. The next degree is what is done for some worldly matter—using good deeds as a means to obtain it.

Finally, [showing off] is that which is done out of fear of the scornful gaze of people.

[It is cured] by knowing that if all of creation were to join forces to oppose you or support you, they would not be able to do so

Except by His permission. Indeed, He alone possesses rewards [for your actions] in both abodes, and He is all-powerful, the Ever-Righteous, and Thankful.

Definition

The next spiritual disease is ostentation (*riyā'*), the most nefarious form of which is when a person performs rites of worship merely to obtain a place in the hearts of others. In plain terms, it is showing off, doing something to gain notoriety. The Prophet ﷺ referred to this behavior as "the lesser idolatry." He also said, "I do not fear that you will worship the sun, the stars, and the moon, but I fear your worshipping other than God through ostentation." He said, moreover, "What I fear most for my community is doing things for other than the sake of God."

Imam Mawlūd outlines three signs of ostentation. The first two are laziness and lack of action for the sake of God when one is alone and out of view of others. When alone, such a person becomes lethargic, unable (or unwilling) to perform acts of devotion, such as reading the Qur'an at home; but in the mosque, in the presence of others, he finds the drive to recite. This is not to suggest that one should not respond to the inspiration one receives when in the company of people who are doing good deeds; the point here is guarding the motivation behind one's acts, especially devotional ones, ensuring that they be for God alone and not for anyone else.

Another sign of ostentation is increasing one's actions when praised and decreasing them in the absence of such praise. In Islamic sacred law, encouragement is not censured. When the Prophet ﷺ saw somebody doing something good, he would say, "You did well." He also said, "When a believer hears somebody praising him, his faith [*imān*] increases," not his pride. He is encouraged to do more for the sake of God, not for the praise. Scholars distinguish between this form of praise and the dishing out of empty flattery. One is encouraged to convey to people that that they have done a job well. This is especially true with young people, as it is important to encourage them to do good.

The root source of ostentation is desire, wanting something from a source other than God. The Imam says that the cure for ostentation is the same as the cure for reckless compromise (*mudāhana*). It is to actively and sincerely seek purification of the heart by removing four things: love of praise; fear of blame; desire for worldly benefit from people; and fear of harm from people. This is accomplished by nurturing the certainty (*yaqīn*) that only God can benefit or harm one. This is at the essence of the Islamic creed. The Prophet ﷺ said:

> Be mindful of God, and God will protect you. Be mindful of God, and you will find Him in front of you. If you ask, ask of God. If you seek help, seek help from God. Know that if the whole world were to gather together to benefit you with anything, it would benefit you only with something that God had already prescribed for you. And if the whole world were to gather together to harm you, it would harm you only with something that God had already prescribed for you. The pens have been lifted, and the ink has dried.

It is astonishing how much energy people expend seeking the pleasure of others, trying, for example, to seek prestige or promotion by pleasing someone in authority. Praise—especially as it is doled out to athletes, musicians, and actors—is almost always ephemeral. And, as it is with the immutable nature of ephemeral existence, the culture of praise is utterly fickle and unworthy of the chase. When a person finds himself with great wealth and fame, friends start to appear everywhere. But if he were to lose his wealth and standing, those friends disappear. Traditionally in the Muslim world, knowledge was the spiritual wealth people wanted to be associated with, not material wealth. It is a remarkable fact about the Muslim world that there were impoverished scholars who achieved great status in the world solely because of their knowledge. Sadly, such is often no longer the case.

Helen Keller once said that there is no slave in this world that did not have a king somewhere in his ancestry, and that there is no king that did not have a slave somewhere in his ancestry. This world has peaks and valleys. Nothing in creation is permanent. To spend time and energy seeking permanence in the fleeting things of the world—like praise—and to neglect what lasts forever with our Maker is the summit of human folly. Hence, one must recognize that there is no harm or benefit except with God, who purifies the heart of vain pursuits and ostentation.

The Imam then discusses another manifestation of ostentation, namely, performing acts of worship in order to be entrusted with the wealth of an orphan and then misusing it for personal needs. This is hypocrisy, one of the most despised characteristics and most damnable. Another offence involving ostentatious display of piety is in the desire for worldly benefit. An example of this is taking advantage of an endowment established for religious purposes and using it for something else. The same is true for any fundraising for religious objectives, which is diverted to other ends. The level of depravity in such fraud is staggering.

A lesser form of ostentation is displaying good works to keep the scorn and criticism of others at bay. This is cured by knowing that God's will cannot be thwarted. Only He possesses the dominion of the heavens and the earth, and only He recompenses people for their actions "in the two abodes," this world and the Hereafter.

POEM VERSES 87–94

[It is also cured] by being always conscious of its harm,
which results in detesting it and thus warding it off.

That is its theoretical treatment. And veiling one's actions
from the eyes of others is its practical treatment,

As is frequent recitation of Sura al-Ikhlāṣ
and the "master supplication for forgiveness."

As for the chronically diseased heart that results from
showing off [one's good works], it too will find a cure in
this, and what a cure!

As for a type of hypocrisy that involves concealing one's
wrong actions or some sexual impropriety, this is in fact an
obligation, as Ibn Zukrī elucidated.

As for what relates to the permissible, adorning oneself
with it falls between recommended and prohibited.

For the seeker of knowledge or someone desiring to show the blessings of wealth, it is recommended; included in this is someone visiting a brother for the sake of God,

Or any other well intended deed for that matter—unless you desire thereby haughtiness or boastful competition. Then it would be considered prohibited.

Treatment

Being aware of the harm associated with ostentation is an effective treatment in itself, since it is human nature to avoid what invites harm. A showoff is invariably discovered, humiliated, and then scorned. And ultimately, he is bankrupt because insincerity is not acceptable to God. This is a "theoretical treatment" that staves off ostentation.

The "practical treatment" involves intentionally veiling one's actions from the eyes of people. This way, one's intentions are protected from vanity. This does not mean that one should never perform deeds in front of people, but that one should also do them when others are not watching. For example, it is good to give money toward charity anonymously. However, giving openly is not a problem if the intention is to encourage others to give as well. The Qur'an praises both, "*Those who spend their wealth by night and by day, secretly and openly*" (QUR'AN, 2:274). Each person is the shepherd of his or her own heart. The night prayer vigil (*tahajjud*), engaging in *dhikr* litanies (remembrance of God), reciting Qur'an, and the like are excellent works to perform in privacy.

It is recommended to recite often Sura al-Ikhlāṣ (the 112th sura of the Qur'an), which affirms the oneness of God and negates the possibility of there being anything comparable to Him. The Arabic word for "sincerity," *ikhlāṣ*, comes from the root *khaluṣa*, which means "to be pure," as in pure honey or pure milk. As for one's piety, it can never be pure unless free of ostentation. In the Qur'an, there are two words that point to sincerity: *mukhliṣ* and *mukhlaṣ*. The latter is the active participle, which indicates that the agent of purification is external;

that is, it is a blessing from God. Imam Ibn Qayyim al-Jawziyyah, a thirteenth century scholar, said that it is possible for anyone to have sincerity in what one does and in what one believes, irrespective of creed. However, being *mukhlaṣ*, purified by God, is reserved for those who have a system of belief and deeds that are concordant with what God has revealed. God loves this kind of human being. Imam Abū al-Ḥasan al-Shādhilī, a thirteenth century scholar, once prayed, "O God, make my bad actions the bad actions of those whom You love, and do not make my good actions the good actions of those with whom You are displeased."

Imam Mawlūd recommends that one repeat regularly a beautiful supplication of the Prophet ﷺ. Known as *sayyid al-istighfār* (the master supplication for forgiveness), it is translated as follows:

> O God, You are my Lord; there is no God but You. You created me, and I am Your servant. I uphold Your covenant and Your promise to the best of my ability. I seek refuge in You from the faults of my own doings. I acknowledge the blessings You have showered upon me, and I acknowledge my shortcomings. So forgive me, for indeed, none forgives sins except You.

The Prophet ﷺ said, "Whoever says this when he arises in the morning and [again] in the evening and then dies either that day or that evening will enter the Garden."

POEM VERSES 95–100

Scholars are of two opinions about seeking some benefit in
this life through worship, as opposed to seeking only
the Hereafter, or even seeking the Hereafter or worship seeking
its delights: Is it sincerity or showing off?

Some also consider that merely taking delight in people's
awareness of one's actions is showing off, though the Star
[Imam Mālik] did not consider that harmful as long as the
original intention was based on the foundation of sincerity.

In fact, deeds that are done while showing off are better than abandoning them out of the fear of [showing off].

Similarly, the scholars have preferred the remembrance of God on the tongue with a heedless heart over a heedless heart and tongue combined!

Discussion

The Prophet ﷺ said that whoever recites everyday the chapter of the Qur'an called al-Wāqiʿah (QUR'AN, 56) will be protected from financial calamity. One of the Prophet's Companions, Ibn Masʿūd, was once asked about what he left his daughters as inheritance, and his reply was that he left them the Chapter al-Wāqiʿah. Imam Mawlūd mentions variant opinions about the issue this raises, namely, seeking worldly benefit through acts of worship, as opposed to exclusively seeking out benefit in the Hereafter. The example here is reciting the sura al-Wāqiʿah with the sole intention of not being impoverished in this world. The hadith is explicit in mentioning the benefit of reciting the sura everyday. But what is the core intention behind this recitation? First, there is always something meritorious and faithful in doing anything related by the Messenger of God ﷺ. Second, reading this chapter is not the same as investing in a worldly venture that more or less shows tangible benefit. Reciting al-Wāqiʿah is seeking benefit from God, the Revealer of the Qur'an. Some have questioned, however, those who recite the Qur'an simply seeking out some worldly benefit, without an eye looking toward the Hereafter; the sura itself describes such people with chilling imagery. Some have gone even further, suggesting that worship even for the sake of reaping the delights of the Hereafter is imperfect worship, since the highest degree of faith entails worship that is solely for the pleasure of God.

Imam Mālik said that to seek out Paradise is more than acceptable, though the motivation behind worship should ultimately be solely for the sake of God and fulfillment of His commands. Some Sufis frown upon the notion of devotions for the sake of worldly benefit, such as reciting Qur'an for the purpose of warding off poverty. It is their conviction that worship is a sacred activity that should be performed strictly in obedience to God's will.

While many Sufis hold this opinion, Qadi Abū Bakr Ibn al-ʿArabī dissents. He says that if one reads the Qur'an and applies the intellect, he or she will readily see that God encourages His creation to strive for Paradise and for deliverance from the Hellfire. Regardless of such authoritative views, one still finds a range of opinions. Rābiʿah al-ʿAdawiyyah once said, "Go after the Gardener, not after the Garden." She also said, "O God, if I worship You for Paradise, then put me in the Fire." This is an extreme statement (*shaṭḥah*) said in a state of spiritual ecstasy. Qadi Abū Bakr and Sīdī Aḥmad Zarrūq say that in no way should anyone belittle the worship of God with the hope of admittance into the Gardens of Paradise, for this is not belittled in the Qur'an.

Imam al-Ghazālī says that there are three types of people: (1) Those who worship God freely (*aḥrār*); they do so only for the sake of God and His pleasure; included in this type are those who are diligent in their worship to fulfill their covenant of obedience to God. (2) The second type is people who worship like merchants (*tujjār*), looking to get something out of their worship; for example, a person of this type prays a certain number of prayers in order to receive a known reward, such as a palace in Heaven. (3) Finally, the third type is those who worship like slaves (*ʿabīd*); they do it out of fear of punishment, specifically, fear of Hellfire. Indeed, the Qur'an does encourage people to race for forgiveness, compete for Heaven, and the like. Many verses describe the terrors of Hellfire so that people will fear it and do all they can to be delivered from it. Many verses also denote the great beauties, rivers, and absolute peace of Paradise. This encourages people to be vigilant in their rites of worship and other obligations in order to reach the stations described so wonderfully in the Qur'an. Qadi Abū Bakr says that having desire for the Garden in the Hereafter or fearing Hell is an expression of *akhlāq*—good, wholesome, and proper comportment—toward God, for people are responding to what God has revealed.

Scholars of shariah say that it is perfectly acceptable to worship in order to seek out the pleasures of the Afterlife, since there is ample encouragement of this in the Qur'an. This is the strongest opinion. Those who proffer dissenting opinions about this matter are among the extremists in the realm of Sufism.

The Imam then speaks of a subtle matter involving people finding pleasure in worship, and how some people are motivated to worship for the purpose of seeking out this pleasure. It is true that when one engages in worship with an open heart and full presence of mind, over time, he or she will discover joy and pleasure in the very act of worship. In fact, this pleasure attained in worship is often described as more pleasurable than the worldly pleasures that preoccupy others. Imam Abū Ḥanīfah said, "If the kings knew the pleasure we are in, they would send their armies with swords to take it away from us." He was referring to the pleasure derived from the worship of God and from gaining knowledge of His religion; kings would leave their palaces and treasures to usurp what the scholars and great worshippers have.

There are people, however, who find this pleasure so compelling that they perform acts of worship for the sake of experiencing it. Some scholars warn against this. Nonetheless, as one scholar said, "Had it not been for these things, most people would have a difficult time worshipping consistently." God has placed pleasure in rites of worship as a reward for their constant practice, for there is a blessing in worship, and seeking it out should not be belittled, since it is from God Himself.

It is interesting that Imam Mawlud mentions these various opinions. He does so, perhaps, to alert the worshipper of what people might say to one who seriously treads the road to finer and more meaningful worship of God.

The Imam then speaks of those who find themselves enjoying the fact that people are becoming aware of their devotional acts of worship. In other words, a person performs an act of worship for the sake of God but is pleased when he finds out that others have learned of it. Some scholars consider this ostentation. According to others, it is not ostentation as long as his intention when performing the act was sincerely for the sake of God. The fact that one likes it when people learn of his devotion is a separate matter from the actual intentions that propelled him to worship in the first place. Scholars say that it is part of human nature to enjoy the good things one does and, in turn, to be pleased when others recognize it. However, if one performs acts of worship for the purpose of receiving praise and recognition, then it becomes blameworthy ostentation. Aḥmad ibn Abī al-Ḥawārī said, "Whoever loves to do something and loves to be known for it has committed idolatry [*shirk*]."

Imam al-Jazūlī said that a person may engage in blameworthy ostentation even if no one is there to notice. For instance, he warns that if a person reads something and comes across some abstruse matter, and thinking it would be good to mention in public, he writes it down or memorizes it, with the intention of preparing for the grand moment to unleash this newfound knowledge before people—this is ostentation and different from learning something so that others may benefit from it.

Scholars in particular are in danger of this kind of ostentation. When scholars gather together, there are certain expectations among them. Becoming preoccupied with this expectation and working to learn something for the sake of peer pressure can turn into a kind of ostentation. A great early scholar named Saʿd ibn ʿAbd Allāh said, "Whoever desires people to know what is between him and his Lord is in a state of heedlessness." Of course, there are exceptions to this. It could be that a worshipper sees that people have abandoned good actions, and so he does them publicly as a way of admonition and as a reminder. For instance, Ibn ʿUmar and Ibn Masʿūd were known to go to the mosque before dawn in order to perform the night vigil prayer (*tahajjud*). They could have performed this voluntary worship in the privacy of their homes, but they did it in the mosque in order to encourage others to do the same.

Next, Imam Mawlūd refers to Imam Mālik as *al-najm* (the Star), for his students used to say, "If we speak of scholars, Imam Mālik is the Star." (Imam Abū Ḥanīfah is called *al-Imam al-ʿAẓam*, the Greatest Imam.) Imam Mālik did not consider that epithet harmful, as long as the original intention was based on the foundation of sincerity. Imam Mālik was once asked, "What do you say about a man who walks to the mosque for the sake of God, but then on the way there thinks to himself, 'I hope someone sees me walking to the mosque'?" Imam Mālik did not see this as harmful as long as the man started out with sincerity and wards off such whisperings.

Imam Mawlūd then says that abandoning a good act out of fear of ostentation is worse than engaging in ostentation itself. A person should not abandon, for example, going to the mosque because he fears ostentation as the motive. One should not submit to an irrational fear that is perhaps inspired by evil whisperings and thus deprive oneself of the blessings of congregational prayer in a mosque. It is better to continue with one's good deeds and to work to keep one's intentions pure and sincere.

If there is an act of worship that one may do in private, then perhaps it is better to do so. As previously mentioned, it is an ethic of Islam that one perform some acts of worship privately in order to train the soul and purify one's intention and guard it from ostentation.

The Imam mentions an interesting fact. Engaging in remembrance of God (*dhikr*) with one's tongue, even if the heart is heedless, is better than abandoning it altogether. What a person repeats on his tongue might eventually reach the heart, even if the heart is not yet engaged, for the heart of man lies under his tongue. (Interestingly, in Chinese medicinal theory, there is a direct connection between the tongue and the heart. Even the movement of the tongue affects the heart.)

The essence of ostentation is being occupied with people instead of God. According to a hadith, the Prophet ﷺ told ʿĀ'ishah that everybody will be naked on the Day of Resurrection. ʿĀ'ishah exclaimed, "Will they not look at each other?" The Prophet ﷺ told her, "The Day of Resurrection will be immensely greater than that!" In other words, people will be in such a state of awe and trepidation, they will not care about seeing anyone. They will only concern themselves with their own souls and salvation.

The essential point about worship is that it should be done purely for the sake of God. When one cleanses the soul of anything that tarnishes one's intentions, one's knowledge of God will increase. As a consequence, everything else in the world will grow insignificant. Imagine how awestruck the Prophet ﷺ must have been when he saw the Angel Gabriel (Jibrīl) ؑ in his true form, his majestic wings filling the horizon. Then, imagine worshipping God, the Eternal, the Infinite, the Glorious. To worship God as if one sees Him is a characteristic of excellence in worship (*iḥsān*), as the Prophet ﷺ taught. Seeking to impress humans is a pathetic exercise, an utter waste of time and life, for humanity is in constant and total need of God. If one wants to be close to power and authority, then one should not chase men of position and station. Rather, one should seek closeness with God, the Master of the universe, the Creator of all things. There is absolutely no power or might except with Him.

Relying on Other Than God

POEM VERSES 101–105

Fear of and desire for other than my Lord contradicts absolute trust in Him. The origin of

Both of them—and I seek refuge in the Mighty from every disease—is lack of certainty.

What is prohibited from the two is that which prevents an obligation from being fulfilled.

As for it leading to the neglect of that which is recommended, then it is considered reprehensible. In any case, flee in fear to your Lord from both of them.

The cure for both is to know that there is none who can bring benefit or harm other than Him alone.

Definition and Treatment

Fearing or desiring anything other than God runs contrary to trust and reliance on God (*tawakkul*). If one is obsessed with other mortals, his or her reliance on God is weak. This diminishes one's certainty (*yaqīn*) in God and certainty that everything good—all that is worthy of pursuit and time—comes from none other than God. The cause of many diseases of the heart can be traced back to a lack of certainty and an impaired sense of faith and trust in God.

A person can be in pursuit of attaining benefit from people and fall into the trap of neglecting his obligations, as well as those meritorious acts that invite untold blessings and dimensions of realization to one's life. One needs to seek refuge in God from the kinds of fear and desire that divert one's attention and striving away from God. The Imam's admonition is to always keep in mind that God alone holds all benefit, and that only God tests people and provides relief and provision.

Displeasure with the Divine Decree

POEM VERSES 106–107

Displeasure with the divine decree occurs when one resists God, the Majestic and Exalted, in what He has decreed.

For instance, saying, "I did not warrant this happening to me!" or "What did I do to deserve this suffering?"

Discussion

The Imam speaks next of "displeasure with the divine decree," a phenomenon that should ring familiar. How many times have we heard a person bemoan, "I do not deserve this!" or "Why me?" or utter such similar statements? Many people live with rancor in their hearts because of what they have been dealt with in life. This attitude toward trials stems from a denial of God's omnipotence and that God alone decrees all things. We cannot choose what befalls us, but we can choose our responses to the trials of life, which are inevitable. His decree is but a command from Him: "'*Be*' *and it is!*" as is repeated in the Qur'an (2:117, 3:47, 6:73, 16:40, 19:35, 36:82, 40:68). Imam Abū Ḥasan said that there is a quality in people that most are unaware of, yet it consumes good deeds: displeasure with God's divine decree (*qadar*).

God-conscious people, when asked about what their Lord has given them, say that all of it is good. They say this out of knowledge of the nature of this world, as a temporary crucible of trial and purification. Because of this elevated understanding, they are patient with afflictions and trials. For worldly people, there is only this world, and this understanding creates a blind spot to the wondrousness of God's creation and His signs strewn throughout.

There are only four possible states in which the human being can live, according to revealed sources. A person is either receiving blessings (*niʿmah*) or *tribulations* (*balāʾ*) from God; or is either living in obedience (*ṭāʿah*) to God or in *disobedience* (*maʿṣiyyah*). Each condition invites a response. When God bestows blessings, the response should be gratitude in all of its manifestations. According to sacred law, gratitude is expressed first by performing what is obligatory (*wājib*), and then going beyond that by performing virtuous, recommended (*mandūb*) acts. Gratitude is an awakening of appreciation in one's heart and an acknowledgement of what one has received. Abusing one's material assets (hoarding them without consideration of the needy or applying them toward forbidden matters) is a flagrant act of ingratitude.

The response to tribulation is patience (*ṣabr*), as well as steadfastness and resolve. This is what God demands from people in times of trial—"a beautiful patience," as close as possible to what Jacob ﷺ exhibited in response to the disappearance of his beloved son Joseph ﷺ and the machinations of his other sons (QUR'AN, 12:18), or to the patience of Job ﷺ during his afflictions.

As for obedience, one must recognize that obedience is a blessing from God. If a religious person starts to believe that he is better than other people—even if these "other" people are in the state of disobedience—he invites haughtiness. This is the danger of obedience and, in fact, the danger of religion: self-righteousness. Imam Ibn ʿAṭāʾallāh said, "How many a wrong action that leads to a sense of shame and impoverishment before God is better than obedience that leads to sense of pride and arrogance!" In this is the secret of wrong actions. The New Testament relates the story of the pride of the righteous Pharisee and the contrition of the humble tax collector. Jesus ﷺ remarks, "Those who make themselves great will be humbled, and those who humble themselves will be made great." Sīdī Aḥmad Zarrūq said that the goodness in obedience is in its essence, and the evil in obedience is what it can result in. This does not mean that there is evil in obedience and goodness in disobedience. Rather, Sīdī Aḥmad Zarrūq points out the danger of obedience creating vanity in one's heart, an aura of sanctimony and condescension. On the other hand, when one indulges in wrongdoing and is overcome with feelings of shame, this can inspire him to hasten to repentance. The Prophet ﷺ said that he feared for his people the vanity of self-righteousness.

The Prophet ﷺ also said that whoever has a mustard seed of arrogance in his heart will not enter Heaven; this sentiment is shared with Christianity. What God asks from obedient people is simply acknowledging that their obedience is a gift from God. The Prophet ﷺ said, "Do not find fault in others. If you find fault in them, God may take their faults away and give them to you." It is unbecoming for a believer to look with scorn at those in tribulation and exhibit a loathsome disdain toward others who seem misguided. It is far better to come with compassion toward them and gratitude to God. When the Prophet ﷺ saw people severely tried, he made the supplication: "Praise be to [God] who has given me wellbeing such that I was not tried like these people. And He has preferred me over so much of his creation." When the Prophet ﷺ witnessed people in tribulation, he responded with compassion for them and gratitude for wellbeing.

When it comes to disobedience (*maʿṣiyyah*), the correct response is sincerely repenting to God (*tawbah*); seeking His forgiveness, pardon, and mercy; feeling remorse for past sins; and having the resolve never to sink into disobedience again.

Everything that can happen to a person falls into one of these four categories, and each invites an appropriate response. What comes to a person in his or her life may help a person move closer to God when the response is right: "*It may be that you dislike something, though it is good for you. And it may be that you love something, though it is bad for you. And God knows, and you do not know*" (QUR'AN, 2:216). Ibn ʿAbbās said that if a person is tested with a tribulation, he will find in it three blessings: firstly, the tribulation could have been worse; secondly, it was in worldly matters and not in spiritual ones; and thirdly, it came in the finite world and not the infinite one. All these are reasons to thank God even for tribulations.

It is important to look at the life of the Prophet ﷺ and to recognize that no one faced greater tribulation. The Prophet ﷺ lived to see all of his children buried, except for Fāṭimah. How many people experience that in their lifetime? Out of six children, he saw five of them perish. His father died before his birth. His mother died when he was just a boy. His guardian grandfather then died. When he received his calling, he saw his people turn against him with vehemence and brutality. People who had once honored him now slandered him, calling him a madman, liar, and sorcerer. They stalked him and threw stones until he bled. They boycotted him and composed stinging invectives against him. He lost his closest friends and relatives, like Ḥamzah. After 25 years of blissful marriage, his beloved wife, Khadījah, died during the Prophet's most trying times. Abū Ṭālib, his protecting uncle, also died. The Prophet ﷺ was the target of thirteen assassination attempts. How many people have faced all of that? Not once in a single hadith is there a complaint from him—except when beseeching his Lord.

To be displeased at God's divine decree is to plunge into heedlessness (*ghaflah*). In his book *al-Furūq*, Imam al-Qarāfī distinguishes the difference between a divine decree and being content with the decree itself. Should people be happy with all that comes their way, including the bad things? God has decreed that evil exist in the world in order to test humankind and for reasons that accord with His wisdom. We should not be displeased with His choice in allowing this. But when one sees societies plunged into immorality, it is not something to be pleased with or even to feel indifferent toward. On the contrary, God requires that we dislike it. But never should we resent or be displeased with the fact that God has created a world wherein such things exist, however unpleasant they may be. As Ibn ʿAbbās said, every trial could have been worse, such as if it involved one's worldly affairs rather than religion, and if it came in this world and not the Hereafter, which lasts forever.

Imam al-Qarāfī gives the example of a physician who amputates the arm of a patient who had gangrene spreading out of control. One day, the physician overhears the patient complaining that the physician was ignorant for amputating his arm. The physician is offended, for he saved the man's life. Had the physician heard the patient praising him—despite the fact that he lost an arm and is discomforted by pain—the physician would feel compassion for the man. So if one speaks about God's decree, saying, "God is testing me, but it is His will and there is wisdom in it," this differs greatly from the remarks of one who complains about the perceived injustices in the world.

Seeking Reputation

POEM VERSES 108–116

[The disease of] seeking reputation entails informing others of one's acts of obedience after they had been performed free of blemishes.

This results from some causes of showing off. A good deed becomes corrupted when telling others of it. But should you repent, [the deed's goodness] is restored.

Similar to this are deeds done so that others may hear about them. The one who does this is also considered a seeker of reputation, according to those with insight.

The great Brigand [al-Shiẓāẓ] who robs all of these wayfarers is covetousness.

This is the cause of every iniquity, such as backbiting, lies, preoccupation of the heart during one's prayers, and insincere praise of others. Indeed, one will inevitably resort to hypocrisy as a result of it.

If you could ask desire itself about his trade he would answer, "Earning humiliation!" or about his father, he would respond,

"Doubt concerning the divine apportioning [of provision]." Or about his objective, he would say, "Deprivation of the very thing one longs for."

Its definition is longing for some benefit from creation. But if one recognizes that [creatures] are incapable of benefiting anyone, even themselves, then [covetousness] wanes.

Discussion

Seeking reputation (*sumʿah*) is a disease of the heart closely related to ostentation. This disease involves desiring that people *hear* of one's goodness, an aural ostentation. It is seeking out renown: for example, a person wanting others to hear how much money he or she gave in charity. The Prophet ﷺ said, "Whoever seeks out reputation, God will expose him on the Day of Judgment." Whomever God debases, none can elevate: "*You exalt whomever You will; and You debase whomever You will. In Your Hand is all good. Indeed, You have power over all things*" (QUR'AN, 3:26).

The Imam says that performing an act for the sake of God is ruined when one goes about informing people of it afterwards. Repentance restores the value of the good deed. Ibn ʿAbd al-Salām states that there is no harm in informing others of one's works for the purpose of encouraging them to do good. But even in this case, one must tread carefully. The hadith says, "Whoever displays his good deeds to others, God will display his bad deeds on the Day of Judgment."

The Imam uses a word here that is taken from the name of a well-known brigand, Shiẓāẓ from Banī Ḍabbah, whose name the Arabs came to apply in a proverb. For example, a notorious thief is called Shiẓāẓ. Metaphorically, coveting renown is the brigand who robs people on the road to their Lord.

The spiritual sage Abū al-ʿAbbās al-Mursī relates that he once was in the marketplace and saw someone he knew, a very righteous man known for his scholarship and spirituality, and who was also a merchant. Al-Mursī, as he relates, thought to himself that if he were to go to this righteous person, he could purchase his goods for a better price because the merchant was an exceptionally religious person and knew what a good man al-Mursī was. But then al-Mursī heard an inner voice admonishing him, "Make your religion sound, and do not desire benefit from created beings." The life-support for ostentation and reputation is covetousness. And the cause of this covetousness, according to Sīdī Aḥmad Zarrūq, is heedlessness (*ghaflah*). A person permits himself to forget that blessings are from God alone. No good or harm can come to one except by God's leave. This level of heedlessness is not a casual lapse of memory. People can become so terribly preoccupied with seeking things from other people that they become heedless of God's power and ownership. When this happens, a person opens his or her heart to all kinds of spiritual diseases. God warns against heedlessness in the Qur'an. To ignore these warnings is the summit of carelessness. "*And if God were to touch you with affliction, there is none who can relieve it save Him. And if He were to touch you with good fortune, then [know] He is powerful over all things*" (QUR'AN, 6:17). The Prophet ﷺ said, "Know that if an entire nation were to gather together to benefit you with anything, it would benefit you only with something that God had already prescribed for you. And if [an entire nation] were to gather together to harm you, it would harm you only with something that God had already prescribed for you."

When the topic of God's power is discussed, questions often arise about those who hold rancor in their hearts to the degree that they wish harm to come to others. There is real concern about the affliction such people can cause. It is necessary to remember that when one is straight with God—observant of His commands, avoiding what He has prohibited, and going beyond the mere obligations by remembering Him often through litanies, voluntary acts of worship, and generosity in charity—the prayers of others to befall one will not prevail. But if one is oppressing people—depriving them of their rights—then one is justified in feeling some fear, for the Prophet ﷺ said, "Fear the supplication of the oppressed." If someone prays against another unjustly, then the iniquity will revert back to the wrongdoer. God never commanded people to supplicate against others, with the exception of the oppressors. God said, "*Let there be no hostility except against oppressors*" (QUR'AN, 2:193). The Prophet ﷺ said that supplication is "the weapon of the believer," a great blessing from God. In many circumstances, we find people bereft of any means to defend themselves against wrongdoing and oppression, and all they have is the power of supplication. But to say "that is all they have" is rather ironic, given there is no power or might except with God. Sincere supplication is very powerful, and God answers the prayers of those who call on Him earnestly. When oppressed, the cries of even an atheist are answered, according to the sound hadith.

Sīdī Aḥmad Zarrūq holds that heedlessness is blindness to the providential order that God has set in place and sustains at every instant. A person may say, after recovering from an illness, "How wonderful is this medication! It saved my life." This is heedlessness of the fact that one of the attributes of God is that He is the Healer. This is not to say that people should not take medicine, but it is important to be aware that it is God who has placed in this world remedies for our bodies, and that every bit of this world is in constant dependence on God. The properties of every chemical are in obedience; they do their work because of God's commands. The heedless forget that God truly holds the heavens and the earth, that He is the Owner and Sustainer of the universe, whatever is seen or unseen, large or minute. The believer who recovers from an illness says, "All praise is for God who has healed me." The difference in responses is the difference between sentience and oblivion.

Imam Mawlūd holds that covetousness is the root cause of many iniquities, like slander. A person who slanders another does so for some perceived gain. He desires, for example, to instill negative thoughts in others toward the victim of his slander. Covetousness can be so overwhelming that it occupies one's mind during prayer. It also leads to insincere praise of others in order to derive some benefit from them. Most salespeople, for example, will say just about anything (lies and flattery) to sell their wares. For this reason the "honest merchant will be raised with the martyrs on the Day of Judgment." The honest merchant does not sacrifice his morality and ethics. If he is successful, he knows his success is from God.

It is interesting to observe in traditional cultures, especially in the Muslim world, that the marketplaces are comprised of rows of businesses dealing with the same product. In America, many would consider it foolish to open a business in proximity to another business already selling the same product. In Damascus, everyone knows where the marketplace for clothing is. There are dozens of stores strung together selling virtually the same material and fashions. Not only are the stores together, but when the time for prayer comes, the merchants pray together. They often attend the same study circles, have the same teachers, and are the best of friends. It used to be that when one person sold enough for the day, he would shut down, go home, and allow other merchants to get what they need. This is not make-believe or part of a utopian world. It actually happened. It is hard to believe that there were people like that on the planet. They exist to this day, but to a lesser extent. They are now old, and many of their sons have not embraced the beauty of that way of doing business.

Today's business culture, on the other hand, has a greater tendency to glorify cutthroat strategies, in which it is not enough to do well. Rather, destroying the competition is encouraged and celebrated. This is covetousness puffed up to an obscene degree. As a result, whole societies are wounded spiritually, for the business culture is never contained only among the merchants but flows through the veins of a nation. The Imam says that for this reason, we need to purify ourselves from vile characteristics, such as covetousness. What makes the process difficult is living in a time when the abnormal is made to seem normal. The Qur'an warns that Satan seeks to adorn things before human eyes so that we do not see things for what they are. Even covetousness is now adorned. It is stripped of the stigma it so rightly deserves; it has now become placed under the rubric of "smart business." The terminology changes, though the essence survives shamelessly. The Prophet ﷺ said, "Competition is the disease of civilizations." The propagation of the philosophy of "us against them" will spare no one, neither "us" nor "them." According to this worldview, everyone is considered "them" to someone else. Unnecessary competition grows into animosity. That is how deep and insidious this disease is. Covetousness leaves one with the feeling of desiring more, which leads to a culture that can never be satisfied.

The Greeks differentiated between types of desire. They had a concept called *eros*, a longing for something, which is never really fulfilled—wanting more and more. The Prophet ﷺ said, "Nothing will fill the mouth of the son of Adam except the soil of his own grave. If he had one mountain of gold, he will only desire a second." The Prophet ﷺ also said, "Two people will never be satiated: seekers of knowledge and seekers of the world." Covetousness, if it is not for God and His religion, will be for worldly things.

Imam Mawlūd next personifies "desire" and says, "If you ask desire itself about his trade," it will answer, "Earning humiliation!" As for its father, it would say, "Doubt concerning the divine apportioning [of provision]," meaning being skeptical about how material provisions are allotted to different people.

The provision that one receives is called rizq. Rarely does God use two very similar names that evoke one attribute. When it comes to provision, God is al-Rāziq and al-Razzāq; both names refer to Him as the Provider. We creatures are known as marzūq, the beneficiaries of God's provision. Some scholars say that provision is anything from which a person derives benefit. Others say it refers to all the material possessions one has. The dominant opinion is the former, since God, the Exalted, says, *"And there is not a creature treading the earth but that its provision depends upon God"* (QUR'AN, 11:6).

God divides the provision of people into two kinds: inner (bāṭinī) and outer (ẓāhirī). The outward provision includes such things as food, shelter, and wellbeing. Inner provision includes knowledge, good character, contentment, and similar qualities. Even the people in one's life (friends, teachers, family, etc.) are considered provision.

Along with the provision that God gives, He also has provided the means (asbāb) by which one must seek out his provision. One person may be in possession of a meal that is meant for another, who then is invited to the former's home for that very meal. So a person never loses anything by feeding a guest. It is a provision meant for that guest, which was already decreed by God.

There should be no confusion about the means of attaining wealth and the wealth itself. When one starts to believe that his or her wealth is in the hands of another person, this creates a breeding ground for diseases, such as coveting what others have, doing whatever it takes to get it, and becoming angry when one does not receive what he or she expects. The Prophet 🙵 said that Angel Gabriel 🙵 disclosed to him, "No soul will die until it completes the provision that was allotted to it." One must trust in God and seek refuge in Him from resorting to illicit livelihood out of fear of not having enough wealth.

False Hopes

POEM VERSES 117–120

Its quick-acting poison is extended false hope, which is assuring yourself that death is a long way off.

This generates hardheartedness and indolence regarding obligations, which leads to inroads to the prohibited.

Regarding the one who is engaged in preparing for tomorrow or writing works of knowledge, [extended hope] is not blameworthy.

As for foreboding its origin, it is ignorance of the fact that the entire affair [of this life] is God's alone.

Discussion

Imam Mawlūd speaks next of a "quick-acting poison" that produces an inordinate attachment to worldly concerns, which is a cause of so many diseases of the heart. This poison is extended hope (*taṭwīl al-'amal*), assuring oneself that death is a long way off—a mental environment that leads people to lead their daily lives as though a long life is guaranteed. The dangers of this delusion are self-evident.

But before speaking about the perils inherent in this malady, it must be said that, in some ways, extended hope is a necessary human condition. Scholars have said that if people did not have hope, no one would have ever bothered planting a single tree. If one was sure that he was going to die very soon, he would not have planted an orchard or had children. There would be no infrastructure for the next generation. However, because human beings do have aspirations, they sow orchards and the like. A famous Persian story speaks of a shah who passed by an old man planting an olive tree, which takes decades to produce good fruit. The shah asked, "Do you believe this tree will be of any benefit to you, old man? You will die before it bears fruit." The old man replied, "Those before me planted and we benefited. We should plant so that others after us might benefit." The shah was so impressed with the old man's concern for the future generations that he rewarded the old man with money. The old man then said to the shah, "You see! The tree has brought me benefit already." The shah smiled and rewarded him again. There is a similar Arab proverb that states, "Before us they planted, and now we eat what they have planted. We too must plant, so that those after us will likewise eat."

Extended hope definitely has its place; in fact, it is a mercy from God that we are capable of it; otherwise, no one would embark on a course of education, for example, or undertake any endeavor that requires years before completion. Taking it a step further, one of the problems of modern society—and the apocalyptic nature of the age we live in—is that people are beginning to lose hope in the future. This is especially true among our youth, many of whom are becoming nihilistic, taking a morbid perspective on the world. We live in a fast-food culture, in which we are led to believe that we need to have everything *now*; it is a culture that causes people to lose a sense of a future worth waiting for. Only recently have we seen the first generation in American history that in many ways will be materially worse off than their parents. Prior to this age, Americans were noted for their cheery optimism about the future.

The extended hope that Imam Mawlūd calls a "poison" is akin to false hope that generates hardheartedness and indolence due to heedlessness of the Hereafter. When one believes that he or she will live for a long time, what ensues is a diminution of pondering one's mortality as well as a sense of independence from God. Fuḍayl ibn Iyāḍ—a great early scholar and a man of asceticism—said that the world is divided into two types of people: felicitous (*saʿīd*) and wretched (*shaqī*). No third category exists. Aristotle, an icon of Western civilization, wrote in his *Ethics* that the goal in life is leisure and happiness, a notion reflected in the Declaration of Independence, which states that people have inalienable rights from God, and among them are life and liberty, which are enshrined in Islam's sacred law as well. Thomas Jefferson added to this, "the pursuit of happiness," which implied leisure. What was originally meant by "leisure" was time to study and meditate on life and pursue true happiness.

For most today, however, happiness is pursued through the acquisition and enjoyment of material goods. The believer, on the other hand, finds happiness in genuine worship—a connection with other-worldiness. The human being is a creature that cannot pursue two things simultaneously, especially when they are on opposite poles of the universe. Islam connects the definition and understanding of happiness with what is permanent and real. According to most religious traditions, true happiness is happiness derived from one's relationship with God and seeking happiness in the Hereafter. This includes living a life that prepares one for this destiny. If one is happy in the next world, this is the greatest possible achievement, regardless of one's material accomplishments in this life. Devotion to God includes the enjoyment of God's blessings, such as family, friends, and recreation.

The Prophet Muḥammad ﷺ made a spectacular supplication: "[O God], if You are not angry with me, then I do not care what You do with me." In other words, "If my life is toilsome and difficult, but I have not incurred Your wrath, then I am happy with that." He is happy because he knows that the real life—the everlasting existence—is in the Hereafter.

A wretched existence is plunging headlong into the materialistic world and having nothing good stored for the Hereafter. No matter how "well off" people appear in this world—regardless of the fine goods that surround them—if they have nothing good in the Hereafter, then they are essentially wretched. Fuḍayl ibn ʿIyāḍ said that there are well known signs of wretchedness. The first is having a hard heart. A man saw the Prophet ﷺ kiss a baby and asked him, "Do you kiss your children?" The Prophet ﷺ said, "Indeed, I do." The man then said, "I have ten children, I never kissed any of them," which was considered and aspect of the pride of being a tough Arab. To that the Prophet ﷺ replied, "There is nothing in my religion for a man whose heart is void of mercy." The Prophet ﷺ also said, "Have mercy on those on the earth, and He who is in heaven will have mercy on you." Scholars have said that if you want to know whether or not your heart is hard, then look at your eye. If it is dry and unmoved to tears, this is an indication of a hard heart. This is called *jumūd al-ʿayn* or "an unmoved eye." A person who has sympathy and softness in the heart is said to have a moistened eye.

The hadith states that the second sign of wretchedness is a lack of modesty or shame. Among the words revealed to humanity are, "If you feel no shame, do what you will."

The third sign is coveting the world. It is said that no one increases his good share in the Hereafter without incurring loss in his worldly affairs, and no one increases his worldly affairs without diminishing or harming his share in the Hereafter. Because the two realms are opposites, an increase in one is a decrease in the other. This does not mean that wealthy people automatically have diminished shares in the Hereafter. There is a Moroccan parable of an ascetic who heard about a learned man, a shaykh, who was beloved to God—a saint. This ascetic came down from his mountain riding a lion to meet the shaykh. He arrived at the shaykh's home and saw that he lived in a palace. The ascetic, who lived in a mountain cave, was shocked at the luxury in which the shaykh lived. The shaykh came out to greet the ascetic, who asked the shaykh, "Where can I put my lion?" The shaykh told him, "Put him in the barn with my cow." The ascetic objected, saying, "He will eat your cow." The shaykh told him, "Don't worry. Just put him in the barn with the cow." The ascetic did as he was told. The two then had a large dinner, though the ascetic was accustomed to eating only dates with water. At night, the shaykh went to sleep, while the ascetic stayed up all night in prayer, annoyed by the snoring of the shaykh he heard through the door. The next morning, the ascetic prepared to leave and went to the barn to retrieve his lion. He did not find his lion because the cow ate it. He then said to the shaykh, "Where is my lion?" The shaykh told him, "Your lion is just like you: it is all outward. You thought my cow was a harmless cow, but she was a lion inside." Outward appearances can fool people.

The last sign of wretchedness is having extended hopes, which we have discussed.

The Egyptian scholar, Shaykh Muḥammad al-Khuḍarī, wrote a biography of the Prophet ﷺ called *Nūr al-Yaqīn (The Light of Certainty)*. He mentioned many of the Companions of the Prophet ﷺ who lost all of their worldly goods, especially those who migrated with the Prophet ﷺ from Mecca to Yāthrib (Medina). But their concern was not the world. The scholar also speaks of the first mosque ever built in Islam. It was at Qubā', which is a town near Medina. He said that the mosque was very simple. In fact, a Muslim today would not recognize it as a mosque because of our modern obsession with adorning the outward appearance of things to the neglect of our inward conditions. The Companions focused their concern toward the beautification of the inward soul and the purification of their heart. The difference in emphasis—between the inward and the outward—is the difference between light and dark.

Imam Mawlūd says that extended hope can generate hardheartedness and indolence regarding one's obligations. This indolence or sloth (*kasl*) shows itself in lassitude concerning matters of the Hereafter, such as fulfilling the obligatory acts of worship and other religious dictates. People find reservoirs of energy when it comes to worldly matters but are overcome with sloth when it comes to matters of the Hereafter. There are people who find excuses for neglecting the prayer—the foundation of spirituality. They claim, for example, that they are exhausted from the day's work. To have time and energy for material concerns and none for the Hereafter is wasting one's life away; its cause is lack of certainty (or having disbelief) in the Hereafter. Ḥasan al-Baṣrī once said that if we were able to see the Muslims who fought at Badr, we would think that they were madmen because of their disregard of the world. "But if these Companions saw the best of you, they would say, 'These people have no character.' And if they saw the worst of you, they would say, 'These people do not believe in the Day of Judgment.'"

A popular saying (often erroneously identified as a hadith of the

Prophet ﷺ) is, "Act for your world as if you will live forever, and act for your Hereafter as if you are going to die tomorrow." Shaykh Bashīr ʿUthmān Bashīr, a contemporary scholar, said that people frequently misunderstand this saying and use it as a justification for working very hard for the world. However, the tradition states that we have forever to take care of our worldly affairs, but we must tend to the Hereafter as if death awaits tomorrow. This implies making even our worldly affairs for the sake of God. The point is not to suggest that a person neglect his work; rather, it speaks to one's intentions, such that one's work in the world does not detract from the Hereafter. The Qur'an says, "*Do not forget your portion of this world*" (QUR'AN, 28:77). There are two ways this can be interpreted. First, do not neglect what God has given you to expend for the Hereafter. Second, do not forget or neglect this world, even though the more important concern is the Hereafter. Both understandings are acceptable. Believers are not anti-worldly in a sense propagated by some Christian theologies. The world is a place God made for us to enjoy but not to the point that we forget our purpose and ultimate destiny.

The Qur'an speaks of certain people who, after a long span of time, became hardhearted and ungodly (QUR'AN, 57:16). When a person suffers the passage of time without consistent and serious reflection about the Hereafter, the world takes hold of his heart more and more, which has a way of making it hard. Those who have hard hearts become corrupt. This dynamic applies to societies as it does for individuals.

Although extended hope can harden hearts, Imam Mawlūd says there are exceptions, like one who is "engaged in preparing for tomorrow or writing works." One is not blameworthy for dedicating years of work for a single end product, like a scholarly work from which many people may benefit. It is one of the highest things a person can do. It is, in fact, a form of perpetual charity (*ṣadaqah jāriyah*), whose reward accrues in favor of its progenitor, even after he or she has died. In cases like this, one is not censured for desiring a long life because one seeks to strive in ways that serve God, His religion, and humanity.

The Prophet ﷺ warned against desiring death, for one "should desire life either to repent and make amends for past iniquities, or if one did much good, to increase his righteous deeds." There is so much optimism and hope in this statement of the Prophet ﷺ. If one's past has been marred with evil, then there is a new day and opportunity to turn things around. God says, "*Good deeds blot out the evil deeds*" (QUR'AN, 11:114). People who recognize the urgency of the human condition and their own impending mortality do not squander their time. They set out doing good deeds, such as spreading knowledge, and this is entirely beneficial. God, the Exalted, says, "*What benefits people shall continue on earth*" (QUR'AN, 13:17). Once, a great scholar who was a source of benefit for many people became very ill. A person came to him and asked him if he was fearful of dying. He said, "No! A verse of the Qur'an says that I will not die yet." The man asked, "Which verse?" He said, "*What benefits people shall continue on earth.*" This kind of hope for a long life is a mercy from God, so that people who bring benefit to others will wish for more opportunity to taste the sweetness of being a harbinger of goodness.

It is no coincidence that those very people who do good and who hope to do more of it are, in fact, those who reflect on death and work for the Hereafter the most, so that the Day of Judgment will be a moment of joy and light for them. It is wise to meditate on death—its throes and the various states after it. For example, one should imagine—while he or she has life and is safe—the trial of the Traverse (*al-ṣirāṭ*) that every soul must pass over in the Hereafter, beneath which is the awesome inferno and the screams and anguish of those evildoers who already have been cast therein.

If athletes include as part of their training the visualization of their sport and mentally picturing themselves going through all the steps required for success, how then can believers fail to visualize what is more important and consequential than sport? People of spiritual elevation prepare themselves psychologically for the ultimate journey. Although death is a sudden severance from this life, one remains conscious in a different way. In fact, the deceased is in a hyperconscious state that makes this life appear like a dream. ʿAlī ibn Abī Ṭālib, may God be pleased with him, said, "People are asleep. When they die, they wake up."

Many of the righteous forebears of Muslim civilization stressed that one should visualize the states of death and the Afterlife: their bodies being washed and prepared for burial, being lowered into the grave, having soil cover them, being questioned by the angels, climbing out of the grave on the Day of Resurrection, and being called to stand in judgment before God, the Exalted. In fact, some of them actually placed themselves in an open grave to feel with greater intensity what awaits them. This may seem like a morbid exercise, but it is effective training that adds spring to one's life and enthusiasm to work for the Hereafter, its peace and bliss. Spiritual masters have long said that if a person is struggling with his appetites, this exercise is a good way of controlling them. Reflecting on death brings sobriety to one's state.

Imam al-Qarāfī differentiates between the hope inherent in the Arabic word *rajā'* and the hope implied by *taṭwīl al-'amal*. The Qur'an praises one who hopes for God and meeting Him in the Hereafter: "*Say [O Muḥammad], 'I am but a man like yourselves, but to whom it is revealed that your God is but one God. So whoever hopes to meet his Lord, let him do righteous deeds and never associate anyone with the worship of his Lord'*" (QUR'AN, 18:110). A famous hadith narrated from ʿĀ'ishah relates that the Prophet ﷺ said, "Whoever loves to meet God is one whom God also loves to meet." And ʿĀ'ishah asked, "O Messenger of God, what about disliking death?" He replied, "It is natural to dislike death, but ultimately meeting God is something the believer seeks and looks forward to." This kind of hope is known as *rajā'*. It is hope coupled with sincere effort to achieve what one hopes for.

It was common among Muslim scholars to discuss the delicate balance between hope and fear. If one is overwhelmed with fear, he enters a psychological state of terror that leads to despair (*ya's*)—that is, despair of God's mercy. In the past, this religious illness was common, but it is less so today because, ironically, people are not as religious as they used to be. However, some of this is still found among certain strains of evangelical Christianity that emphasize Hellfire and eternal damnation. One sect believes that only 144,000 people will be saved based on its interpretation of a passage in the Book of Revelations.

Nonetheless, an overabundance of hope is a disease that leads to complacency and dampens the aspiration to do good since salvation is something guaranteed (in one's mind, that is). According to some Christian sects that believe in unconditional salvation, one can do whatever one wills (although he or she is encouraged to do good and avoid evil) and still be saved from Hell and gain entrance to Paradise. This is based on the belief that once one accepts Jesus as a personal savior, there is nothing to fear about the Hereafter. Such religiosity can sow corruption because human beings simply cannot handle being assured of Paradise without deeds that warrant salvation. Too many will serve their passions like slaves and still consider themselves saved. In Islam, faith must be coupled with good works for one's religion to be complete. This does not contradict the sound Islamic doctrine that "God's grace alone saves us."

There is yet another kind of hope called *umniyyah*, which is blameworthy in Islam. Essentially, it is having hope but neglecting the means to achieve what one hopes for, which is often referred to as an "empty wish." One hopes to become healthier, for example, but remains sedentary and is altogether careless about diet. To hope for the Hereafter but do nothing for it in terms of conduct and morality is also false hope.

A perennial teaching of revealed religion since the time of Adam is that entry into Paradise is a matter of God's mercy, which is attained by combining faith with sincere deeds that confirm one's profession of faith. Unfortunately, on the Day of Judgment, many Muslims may find themselves in Hell because of false hopes. All they have to show for their religiosity is the mere declaration of faith, a testimony unconfirmed by deeds, especially the rites of worship and charitable acts toward others.

Fear (*khawf*) treats or prevents two maladies: moral complacency and self-righteousness. Having a good measure of fear is necessary to stay on the path. But when one reaches his or her deathbed, one should have absolute hope in God, and have certainty that God will offer forgiveness and allow him or her entrance into Paradise. This is having a good opinion of our Lord. The Prophet ﷺ warned that no one should die except with "a good opinion about God."

Imam al-Haythamī relates that having extended hope (*taṭwīl al-'amal*) is founded on heedlessness of the reality of death, which, he said, is not wrong in and of itself. There is no commandment that obliges the remembrance of death, although it is difficult to imagine a spiritual life without such reflection. The Prophet ﷺ said, "Remember death" and he said, "I used to tell you do not visit graves, now I tell you to visit graves because it will remind you of the Hereafter." Although these commands do not rise to the level of obligation, they are considered highly recommended (*mandūb*), the same way that the remembrance of God beyond what is prescribed is recommended but not obligatory per se.

The Qur'an states that there are people who desire to continue in their wrongdoing throughout the entirety of their lives. They ask, "*When will this Day of Resurrection come?*" (QUR'AN, 75:6). One interpretation of this verse, according to scholars, is that although people may be aware of ultimate accountability, they put off repentance as if they are guaranteed a long life. This is an ethic exemplified by the saying, "Sow your wild oats," which advocates getting all the lewdness and sin out of one's life when one is young, and then later calming down and adopting religion. Besides the obvious error of this ethic, another terrible flaw is that people die at all ages, and some never get the chance to repent and make amends. Moreover, what kind of repentance is this when people intentionally indulge in sin banking on the possibility that later on in life—after all the energy and drive diminishes—they will turn in penitence to God? We know that God loves those who spend their youth obedient to Him and His commandments.

Imam Mawlūd mentions next the concept of divination and foreboding (*taṭayyur*). When the pre-Islamic Arabs needed to decide upon something, they would run toward a flock of birds. If the flock veered to the left, they took this to be a bad omen; if to the right, it was a good omen.

Foreboding is blatant superstition. The Arabic word *mutaṭayyir* Arabic refers to someone who is a pessimist, who always sees the worst in any given situation. Imam Mawlūd says that superstition is lack of knowledge that everything belongs to God. All affairs are His. Having a good opinion of God produces a view of Him that is impregnable to negative thoughts and behaviors that thrive in the soil of disbelief. To hang on to superstitions is to have a negative understanding of the reality of God and His authority and presence.

There are two types of foreboding. One is based on normative experience: observing things that consistently happen. For example, getting near a cobra usually results in it striking the person. Hence, if one sees a cobra, one should get out of the way. There is no superstition in that. But this differs completely from some practices like avoiding walking under a ladder, staying clear of a black cat, and the culture that has evolved around the number 13 and its association with bad luck. Similar is the stigma connected with breaking a mirror. Even the seemingly harmless "knock on wood" originates from pagan practices of worshipping trees. These superstitions emanate from having a bad opinion of God, not recognizing His power and authority in the world, attributing power to inanimate objects, and delving into other similar practices. Such superstitions are explicitly forbidden in Islam.

What the sacred law permits as a means to avoid calamities is not superstition. Saying certain prayers, reading certain passages of the Qur'an that ward off evil, giving extra charity, and the like are acts of worship. These are based on revelation from God Himself and, therefore, differ completely from pre-Islamic practices, such as avoiding coming between two sheep, which was considered bad luck.

The Prophet ﷺ warned against superstition, no matter how widespread it may be in societies. Some people routinely read the astrology page of the newspaper before starting their day. Often, people buy and sell stocks based on the advice of their astrologers. No matter how common this has become, it remains an offense against revealed religion and God Himself. It is founded on a completely absurd premise. While these practices have taken on an aura of innocence and light humor, they are nonetheless connected to their pagan and idolatrous ancestry.

According to Imam Mawlūd, the way to cure this trap of superstition is for one to simply persist in what one was doing before being confronted with whatever it is that is viewed as a bad omen. Altering one's course of action because of some perceived bad omen is admitting that the superstition has power. It is important to note that if it is not one's habit to have such bad forebodings and one finds oneself with a bad feeling about a situation or person, it is prudent to "listen to the heart." This is known as *firāsah* in Arabic, and in traditional theology is recognized simply as "discernment." It is an angelic agent that attempts to protect us from some imminent harm.

Negative Thoughts

POEM VERSES 121–124

Some assumptions are not permissible, such as holding a bad opinion about someone who manifests righteous behavior.

This means that your heart is convinced and you have judged him based on your heart's suspicions without proof that warrants such an assumption.

There is nothing wrong with having doubts about someone or having a bad opinion of him, if it is based on sound reasoning and is not arbitrary.

Thus, our bad opinion of some profligate whose actions indicate his [corruption] is not prohibited.

Discussion

Imam Mawlūd speaks of something that is very easy to have but is harmful to brotherhood and injurious to one's own spiritual growth. It is having a bad opinion about others, baseless assumptions, and suspicion (*ẓann*). This is allowing conjecture into one's heart without having any facts, which is especially harmful when one harbors a bad opinion about people who are outwardly righteous in appearance, which was something that the early Muslims considered important.

Scholars have advised that one should even beware of forming conclusions based on the bad appearance of people, for it could be that God veiled their goodness from others. The Arabs traditionally were keen on having the ability to see a person's inner goodness. Once an Arab man came to the Prophet ﷺ to see who he was. When the man left, some men asked him about his opinion of the Prophet

ﷺ, and he said, "His face is not the face of the liar." This *firāsah* is, again, having the intuitive ability to see in people signs of goodness or evil. The Prophet ﷺ had this ability to the utmost degree and said that believers possess it also, but to a lesser extent. Sīdī Aḥmad Zarrūq said that every believer has the power of *firāsah* to variant degrees based on the strength of his or her faith.

However, having a bad opinion of someone without cause is considered a malady of the heart: "*O you who believe, avoid suspicion, for some suspicion is sinful*" (QUR'AN, 49:12). Often associated with this disease is backbiting (*ghībah*), that is, speaking ill of another person behind his or her back. It is possible to backbite in an unspoken form, as when a person has unfounded negative thoughts against another person. Suspicion in the heart that affects one's thoughts and opinion of another person is considered backbiting of the heart (*ghībat al-qalb*). This also is not permissible. The Prophet ﷺ said, "Beware of a bad opinion, for it is the most false of speech." If someone says to you that a given person is bad, ask for proof. Without proof, it is tantamount to a lie. The sacred law of Islam (shariah) is based on proof and not conjecture.

Imam Mawlūd says next that having doubts about someone's character is not forbidden if it is based on reason and observable evidence. This is different from suspicion that tends to be judgmental and, oftentimes, specious. God says, "*O you who believe, if an ungodly person brings you some news, then seek out its veracity*" (QUR'AN, 49:6). If someone known to openly indulge in major sins comes with some news, one should not accept it without circumspection. Sīdī Aḥmad Zarrūq gave good advice centuries ago that still remains relevant: "Do not trust anyone with matters related to your religion, your family, or your wealth until you have tested him at least a thousand times." According to this advice, one should test someone's sincerity and trustworthiness before entrusting him with anything significant. If there is much corruption in a given generation, it is best to be wary of people until their goodness becomes manifest. This is the advice of the scholars. There are many people who have no qualms about deceiving and cheating people. They will adorn their faces with smiles and communicate that they are wonderful people, but they will cheat a person when the opportunity arises.

Scholars also say that one should be circumspect with the dispensation of zakat. In times in which goodness prevails over corruption, the default is to accept the word of people who claim they qualify for zakat and ask for it. However, when corruption and fraud are prevalent, then those responsible are obliged to be rigorous in their investigation. Unfortunately, some people will often present themselves as mired in poverty, though they are well off. Charity is considered a trust from God, and its dispensation must be done with care.

Having doubts about people is different from decidedly judging them negatively. Forming a bad opinion in the presence of ample evidence is common sense. However, when people repent, they should not have their past held against them. A hadith says, "There are two things no believer has been given anything better than: a good opinion of God and a good opinion of the servants of God." According to sacred law, people are innocent until proven guilty. This relates to having a good opinion of God. A hadith states that God says, "I am in the opinion of My servant. If he thinks well of Me, he finds good, and if he thinks ill of Me, he finds evil." Another hadith states, "If [someone] finds good, let him thank God, and whoever finds other than that, let him blame only his own soul." The Prophet ﷺ also said that the affair of believers is all good. Even if something unpleasant occurs, there is good in it.

Vanity

POEM VERSES 125–127

Vanity is the aggrandizing of some blessing while forgetting that it came from God.

Treat it by realizing that the Exalted is the Fashioner and the Bestower of blessings,

[Realizing] that because of your impotence, you can produce neither benefit nor harm. Indeed, vanity originates from one's ignorance of these two matters.

Definition and Treatment

The next disease of the heart is vanity, known in Arabic as *ʿujb*, which is related to arrogance. According to Imam al-Ghazālī, arrogance requires two people for its outward manifestation: the arrogant one and the one to whom the arrogance is shown. The possessor of vanity, on the other hand, does not need a second person, as he is impressed with himself; he admires his own talents, possessions, looks, and status, and he considers himself better than others. He exults, for example, when looking at himself in the mirror or gazing upon his accomplishments or property. Imam Mawlūd says *ʿujb* is a nefarious kind of vanity in which a person rejoices in the blessings he has but forgets the source of these blessings.

The fact that someone has talent and is able to develop it into a higher skill or craft and achieve remarkable things does nothing to diminish the obvious—it still is a gift from God. It is part of the sunnah of God in creation, that divine order woven in the fabric of existence, that one must toil to refine his or her skills or talent. A calligrapher, for example, makes his craft appear easy to the onlooker, but one does not see the years of tireless preparation, perseverance, and repetition to master the curves of one letter of the Arabic alphabet and then whole words. On top of that, consider the various styles of calligraphy that the great Muslim calligraphers have developed over the centuries. There are plenty of talented and refined artisans of the world who deem their work astonishing and magnificent. They think only of their long training and deceive themselves into thinking, "I worked so hard, and I did this all by myself." Similarly, one often finds businessmen truly talented and bold in building business, but who admire themselves and extol their financial prowess. Undoubtedly, this invites illness into the heart, for it is God who is the bestower of success and talent.

Imam al-Bayhaqī relates a statement of the Prophet ﷺ in which he said, "God makes every maker and what he makes." In reality, God is the creator of the marvels that people admire and attribute to the glory of humankind, forgetting that it is God who created the ones who produced these marvels. Realizing that God is the source of all blessings prevents vanity from entering the heart.

A person will always find someone with more talent and more knowledge. Ultimately, "*Above all those who have knowledge is the All-Knowing*" (QUR'AN, 12:76), God. Moses عليه السلام was once asked if he was the most knowledgeable of people, and he answered "Yes." Moses عليه السلام was then told that there was a man who had knowledge that Moses عليه السلام did not have. This man was Khiḍr عليه السلام, who was not a prophet, but Moses عليه السلام, without a trace of vanity, became his student. (The story is told in Sura al-Kahf of the Qur'an.)

The word "vanity" comes from the Latin word *vanus*, which means "empty," implying that the source of our vanity is void of substance and will vanish. When the Roman emperor triumphed in a battle, he put on a victory celebration in which the general of the battle paraded through the street. Behind him on his chariot a slave would hold a victory laurel and whisper in the general's ear, "All is vanity," thus reminding the general of the perils of vanity. It is part of ancient wisdom to remind people that all accomplishments people praise and admire will perish until no one remembers them. Charles Lindbergh, the first pilot to successfully fly across the Atlantic, was celebrated as a great hero for his famous flight. Within ten years, however, he was vilified as a criminal by the American press, which falsely claimed that he was a Nazi sympathizer.

How many times have we seen major cities holding massive celebrations for the accomplishments of their sports teams, the huge parades and the hubris tradition of human glorification? How many of these celebrations end up in riots, vandalism, and even loss of life? What about the urban social morass that exists before, during, and after the celebrations? To celebrate in this way is vintage vanity.

There is foolishness in being vain about what one has accomplished, given its ephemeral nature. But when one is thankful to God and acknowledges and praises Him as the source of this goodness, then the accomplishment outlasts our earthly lives and memories of people, for God preserves it.

Vanity originates from one's ignorance of two matters: God alone is the Fashioner and the Giver of Blessings, and we human beings are incapable of accomplishing anything without God's will and blessings. If one accomplishes something, one should remember God and be grateful, and not swagger with haughtiness, for if we do not humble ourselves, God will humble us. When men and women are blessed with exceptional outward beauty, they introduce ugliness when they have vanity for it. When the Prophet ﷺ saw a reflection of himself—and he was a beautiful man—he would make the following supplication: "O God, as You have made my countenance most excellent, make my character most excellent." Imam Mawlūd says that to rid oneself of vanity or to prevent it from entering one's heart, one should reflect long and hard on the fact that all blessings are entirely from God and that one cannot produce any benefit or harm without His permission.

Fraud

POEM VERSES 128–129

Fraud is to conceal some fault or harm, either religious or worldly, even from one who is part of a protected minority,

Or from someone who has a treaty with Muslims. Others have interpreted [fraud] to be the embellishment of something that lacks any real benefit.

Discussion

The next disease is fraud (*ghish*). It is concealing from people some fault, blemish, or harm, either of a religious or worldly nature. Others have said that fraud is making something useless or defective seem useful and beneficial, or making something bad appear to be good. One of the most widely transmitted hadith in the Islamic tradition is the Prophet's saying, "Whoever defrauds us is not one of us." Sacred law forbids selling something without pointing out its defects. If the seller conceals defects or fails to disclose them intentionally, this is fraud, whether its victim is a Muslim or not.

The Sophists of ancient Greece loved and practically worshipped rhetoric. They were the first historical relativists in that they held the theory that right and wrong do not exist in an objective and transcending sense, and that whoever makes the most skilled and persuasive argument is right. The Sophists believed that the most important thing is to be convincing, regardless of whether one is telling the truth or lying, or whether one is defending corruption or upholding justice. This is fraud of the tongue.

Rhetoric was also an art form in Islamic literary and oratory history. But to the Muslim, rhetoric was the art of embellishing the truth and presenting it persuasively.

Anger

POEM VERSES 130–137

As for the swelling ocean of all of these diseases, I mean anger; if you come to its shore, you will see great astonishments.

Its waves and everything else about it are overflowing. So say of it what you will without constraint.

It has two treatments: one of them removes it altogether without trace. The other suppresses it should it manifest itself.

To be adorned with the ornament of its cure, remember the extensive praise lavished upon forbearance and humility,

In sacred law, as well as in the poetry and prose of the wise. Indeed, remember that all of the prophets have been depicted as having both qualities.

Repel [anger] by perceiving at its onset that there is no one doing anything in reality except the Almighty;

Also by performing ablution with cold water, keeping silent, lying down [if one is sitting],

And sitting [if one is standing]. It will pass by doing these things, and also by seeking refuge in God as was mentioned in the tradition.

Anger

Definition

Imam Mawlūd says of the next disease that it is a "swelling ocean." He refers to intense anger or wrath (*ghaḍab*), which aptly compares with a swelling mass of emotion that is difficult to hold back once it is unleashed. Anger is truly an amazing phenomenon if one reflects on its nature and presence in human life and character, its peril and liability, as well as its utility and necessity. According to a hadith, a man asked the Prophet ﷺ, "What is the worst thing that one incurs concerning God?" The Prophet ﷺ replied, "His wrath." The man then asked, "How do we avoid it?" The Prophet ﷺ said, "Do not become angry." This statement reveals a fascinating reality in which we live and informs a good portion of the Muslim religious perspective: there is a correlation between what a person does and what he receives from God in kind—a correspondence that our all-wise Lord has placed in the workings of creation. If one wishes not to incur the wrath of God, then one should not be wrathful or angry with people unjustly. Similarly, the Prophet ﷺ said that whoever makes someone's path to knowledge easy, God will make his or her path to Paradise easy. And whoever covers the shortcomings of his brother, God will cover his shortcomings in the Hereafter. God, the All-Wise, placed this special reciprocity in this world.

Another man asked the Prophet ﷺ, "Give me advice." The Prophet ﷺ said, "Do not become angry." The man asked again, and the Prophet ﷺ repeated his advice. For a third time, the man asked the question, and the Prophet ﷺ said again, "Do not become angry." The repetition of this counsel stresses the importance of the Prophet's admonition about anger. Scholars agree, however, that this hadith does not prohibit anger categorically, for even the Messenger of God ﷺ became angry when appropriate. He once said, "I am a human being, and I become angry like you." The Prophet's anger could be seen on his face. But his anger was always in response to an aberration in human character and behavior offensive to God. So anger is not necessarily a negative emotion in and of itself. It is part of the human creation, just as our flesh and limbs are. Without anger, there are many things that would not have been achieved. Anger can be a positive motivator.

However, there is another side to anger that we must guard against. If it is not guided to something useful, it can possess, consume, and ultimately destroy a person. How many times have we seen or heard of a person who ruined his or her life because of a rash act or statement made in a fit of rage? How many people do we know who are entirely estranged and avoided because of their inability to corral their anger? How many times have people been deeply offended and unjustly violated by the anger of another? How many people create oppressive environments because of the fear they instill in others around them because of irrational and feral anger? Interestingly, Mawlānā Jalāluddīn al-Rūmī locates the wisdom of the Islamic prohibition of alcohol within the peril of anger; when people drink, even if they are not visibly inebriated, they often become easily angered and belligerent. What is mercifully veiled in human beings is often exposed when alcohol enters the scene.

According to scholars, like Imam al-Nawawī and others, when the Messenger of God ﷺ said, "Do not become angry," he meant do not allow anger to lord over oneself and cause the loss of one's comportment. In other words, do not become anger, its embodiment, such that people only see your rage. Instead, control anger and never lose control. Scholars have likened anger to a hunting dog: without training, it will never retrieve what its owner needs nor will it point a person in the right direction. So anger is something that needs to be trained, not abolished, for if people completely suppressed their sense of anger, many of the injustices of the world would not have been opposed and tyranny would have gone unchecked. Without anger, people would go around with complete impunity and commit heinous acts without resistance from the people. Corruption would cover the face of the earth.

Muslim scholars have identified four essential qualities in human beings, which have been identified in earlier traditions as well. Imam al-Ghazālī and Fakhruddīn al-Rāzī adopted them, as did Imam Rāghib al-Isfahānī in his book on ethics. According to Imam al-Ghazālī, the first of them is *quwwat al-ʿilm*, known in Western tradition as the rational soul, which is human capacity to learn. The next one, *quwwat al-ghaḍab*, which may be called the irascible soul, is the capacity that relates to human emotion and anger. The third element, *quwwat al-shahwah*, known as the concupiscent soul, is related to appetite and desire. The fourth power, *quwwat al-ʿadl*, harmonizes the previous three powers and keeps them in balance so that no one capacity overtakes and suppresses the others.

In Western tradition, these capacities correspond to what is known as cardinal virtues. Muslims call them *ummahāt al-faḍā'il*. They are wisdom, courage, temperance, and justice (*ḥikmah*, *shajāʿah*, *ʿiffah*, and *ʿadl*). When the rational soul is balanced, the result is wisdom. Whoever is given wisdom has been given much good (QUR'AN, 2:269). Wisdom, according to Imam al-Ghazālī, is found in one who is balanced, who is neither a simpleton nor a shrewd, tricky person. If there is a deficit in the rational soul, the result is foolishness. When the rational soul becomes excessive and inordinately dominant, the result is trickery and the employment of the intellect toward the exploitation of others.

Courage manifests when the irascible soul—anger—is under control, when a mean is struck between impetuousness (irrational behavior that people ultimately regret) and cowardice, which is marked by fear overriding the anger required to courageously respond to exploitation, oppression, personal threats, and wrongdoing. There is a middle path between these extremes, as the Prophet ﷺ said, namely, a middle way of wisdom and courage.

Temperance (*ʿiffah*) is a balance within the concupiscent soul, which is related to appetite and desire. Those who do not possess this quality often recognize a dignifying quality, a richness of soul of those who do possess it (QUR'AN, 2:273). People of *ʿiffah* tend to abstain from trying to attain wealth, not only through ruse and fraud, but also through begging. Attaining things through illicit means is working from a posture of imbalance with regard to one's desire. It is a suspension or retraction of balance resulting in defrauding people and, ultimately, one's own soul. This is the irony of giving in to one's base desires, which offers some immediate gratification but harms the soul and dampens its spirituality.

The topic of anger is usually treated as a matter requiring balance and is closely associated with those deeds and habits that either throw one's balance off or guard it. As it is traditionally understood, imbalance in one aspect of life affects other areas of human behavior. The Prophet ﷺ said, for example, "The worst vessel the son of Adam fills is his stomach." We understand from this that there is a relationship between character and consumption, a dialogue that the modern marketing desperately wants us to discount. Not only do we oppress our health when we fill our stomachs, but other aspects of our lives are also affected when we do so because of the connection between excessiveness in one area and the corollary damage it brings about in others. Muslim scholars throughout our history have pointed this out and have relied on sound statements of the Prophet ﷺ for proof, for he prayed against a stomach that is not easily satisfied. He recommended that one–third of the stomach be filled with food and one–third with water, and that the last third be left for air.

The same ethic applies to the sexual appetite, which is required for a healthy state. It is discouraged to completely ignore one's desire. But if one transgresses and goes beyond what is permissible, this is oppression and wrongdoing. Popular culture has placed an emphasis on illicit sexual intimacy and recklessness, making it seem normal and acceptable. Sexual relationships between unmarried partners, who neither commit their lives to each other nor feel any necessary emotional ties, is made to seem the summit of sexual excitement.

According to Imam al-Ghazālī, the one who perfected the balance between these forces was the Messenger of God ﷺ, for he was the most just of men. The more one emulates him in his behavior, the greater balance one will achieve. The way of the Prophet ﷺ was the middle way, the way of moderation.

With regard to anger, Imam al-Ghazālī says that it is acceptable only at the right time, in the right place, for the right reasons, and with the right intensity. The Messenger of God ﷺ never allowed his anger to get the best of him. He was in control of himself, secure, and always in the state of spiritual certainty. Out of the thousands of reports about the minutest details of the Prophet's life ﷺ, never has anyone related that the Prophet ﷺ ever did anything that was imprudent or rash. Never did he apply his intellectual gifts and prophetic status for anything other than guiding humanity aright.

Qadi Ibn al-ʿArabī, in speaking about courage and the larger issue of balance, said that after the Messenger of God ﷺ, no one was more courageous than Abū Bakr رضي الله عنه. If one were to ponder the events during the life of the Prophet ﷺ, it was Abū Bakr رضي الله عنه who continually showed up in the Prophet's defense and support. He was particularly firm and resolute, the one who did not waver when others wavered. He was the one who accompanied the Prophet ﷺ in his migration to Medina. Each of the Rightly Guided Caliphs (al-Khulafāʾ al-Rāshidūn) embodied one of the aforementioned virtues as his dominant character. ʿUmar ibn al-Khaṭṭāb رضي الله عنه is associated with being particularly sensitive to justice and fairness. ʿUthmān ibn ʿAffān's name is derived from the same Arabic root as *ʿiffah*, which according to *al-Qāmūs* of al-Fayrūzabādī, refers not only to moderation but also to one who is abstinent and chaste, a meaning that is fitting for ʿUthmān. The Prophet ﷺ once said that even the angels were shy before ʿUthmān because of his modesty. In ʿAlī ibn Abī Ṭālib, there is extraordinary wisdom or *ḥikmah*. It is true that these great heroes of Islamic civilization embodied in a particular way one of the four virtues, but they also kept a balance that enshrined the rest.

The phrase *ṣirāṭ al-mustaqīm*, the straight or upright path, is repeated many times each day by the Muslim worshipper. No phrase better epitomizes the way of life of the Muslim. The word *mustaqīm* suggests balance. If one deviates from this balanced path, he does so in one of two ways: deficiency in fulfilling one's obligations and excessiveness therein. The concept of monkhood, for example, does not receive approbation in Islam as a form of practice. The Qur'an states that the institution of monasticism was not prescribed by God (QUR'AN, 57:27). According to Qur'anic commentators, the people of monasticism became immoderate in their practices, which originated from the desire to gain God's good pleasure. However, they were unable to maintain their practices, which is the nature of excess and its main defect. When one is unable to keep up with certain practices, one becomes either worn out or altogether jaded, and this is antithetical to the straight path of Islam. Balance, then, is not merely a merciful device for adherents, but the shortest distance between a person and his or her spiritual objectives.

The objectives of the rites of worship and practices cannot exceed what is natural. Sexual attraction, like hunger, cannot be removed from the soul; nor is it to one's benefit to try to do so. Celibacy is not considered a virtue in Islam. Chastity and licit sexual intimacy are. Church history tells of the Puritans who went so far as to swear off normal desires, such that sexual relations were nearly tabooed between a man and his wife. It became an entirely perfunctory activity of marriage fleeced of the enjoyment that a husband and wife are not only entitled to have but are encouraged to experience.

The usual result of excessiveness is its antithesis. A society that starts out with extreme Puritanical ethics may turn into one of over-indulgence and licentiousness. On an individual level, the experience is similar. It is a principal feature of the Islamic faith that the "middle way" be the path that Muslims adhere to. The Qur'an itself calls the believers a "middle nation," which commentators say includes moderation, which leads to a consistency of worship and conduct that one can carry on throughout his or her life. It is said that the Judaic legal tradition is based on stern justice, while at the foundation of the Christian phenomena is the idea of categorical mercy where everybody should be forgiven no matter what. With Islam, a balance is struck suitable for the complex societies that have spread across the face of the earth, a balance between avoiding God's *ghaḍab* (wrath and stern justice) and hoping for God's *raḥmah* (mercy). To take the straight way, one must have both, the law and the spirit of the law, the *sharīʿah* and the *ḥaqīqah*. The law consists of rules, and the spirit of the law is mercy. God sent down the shariah as a mercy, and the Prophet ﷺ himself is "*a mercy to the worlds*" (QUR'AN, 21:107).

There is an inward and outward state in every human soul, with the inward being *imān* (the condition of the faith) and the outward being *islām* (the manifestation or practice of the faith). When the two come together inwardly and outwardly, the resulting balance is a truly beautiful human being, one generally called a *muḥsin*, one whose worship and character are excellent. This is the taker of the straight path and what we all strive for and petition God for each time we stand in prayer. According to Ibn al-Taymīyyah, Muslims can deviate by way of striving to avoid God's *ghaḍab* or by way of seeking His *raḥmah*. They may go the way of the hairsplitting, tyrannical scholar who condemns practically everyone and every act, or the way of the ignorant worshipper, as in extreme Sufism, which concludes that all is one and that everybody is going to Paradise, regardless of one's creed, one's disfigurement of God's revelations, and one's outright fabrications about God and His nature.

The balance is to cling outwardly to the law and carry the spirit of Sufism inwardly, as Imam al-Shāfiʿī advised. When Muslims deal with one another, they should incline toward clemency and mercy, not wrath and severity. God says that the former is closer to *taqwah* (God-consciousness) than the latter (QUR'AN, 5:8). It is a more elevated act to reprieve than it is to exact justice. Imam Rāghib al-Isfahānī said, "When love exists, there is no need for justice." What he meant by this is that when love is present and is allowed to override one's anger, the demand for retribution is quieted. If we were to look at the emotions behind the first major trial of the Islamic community after the passing away of the Prophet ﷺ, there was a deviation from the spirit of love and cooperation. Muʿāwiyah ؓ demanded justice for the murder of ʿUthmān ؓ. But ʿAlī ibn Abī Ṭālib ؓ, who had great wisdom, demanded forgiveness because he saw that the demand for retribution would rip the nation apart. Sunni Muslims, however, maintain a good opinion of Muʿāwiyah ؓ, contrary to the Shiites. Sunnis believe his intentions—like those of ʿĀ'ishah and Zubayr ؓ—were purely for the attainment of justice. Imam ʿAlī's position, according to many Muslim historians and scholars, was actually the higher level of Islam, which is to have *raḥmah* or mercy and clemency. What we learn here is that there is hidden hazard in inordinate demands for justice and retribution. As noted above, we have seen how this extreme position can lead to injustice. Extremism, in general, usually results in the opposite extreme. Our early history bears this out, for Imam ʿAlī ﷺ was a victim of injustice by those who rebelled against him out of their sense of indignation.

The cardinal virtues originally stem from religion. A generous person gives from his wealth to others because he is not afraid of losing his power or wealth; he knows all power and wealth are with God. All further virtues emanate from the cardinal virtues (or matrices of virtues). Mercy, for example, issues from wisdom (*ḥikmah*), since forgiving someone when you are wronged requires a recognition of the greater wisdom in remission and the greater good in clemency.

Anger (*ghaḍab*) remains an essential quality of the human creation. The human brain is said to be a triune brain because it has three dominant centers. This observation of the brain is not modern, for Imam al-Ghazālī mentioned it. The lowest brain is known as "R" brain (reptilian according to the evolutionary scheme of things), which is associated with appetite, mainly, for food and sex. The midbrain is where the emotions are centered, which includes anger. The third portion of the brain is known as the new brain or the neo-cortex, which is where the rational faculty resides. When these three centers function properly in proportion to one another, the human being is said to be functioning in equilibrium. Such persons are stable and immediately likeable.

There are people who are almost entirely cerebral; everything is theoretical or abstract to them. Their rational center suppresses their emotions residing in the midbrain and the physical needs in the R-stem. On the other hand, there are people who work mainly from their so-called reptilian centers, almost impervious to protocol, higher ethics, and a civil association with others. It is not unusual to hear someone likening another's behavior to that of a snake, a kind of slinking predator, entirely selfish and wholly tenacious in acquiring his desires. Furthermore, there are people who are overly emotional. They are either very happy or very angry, the latter of which is the more common emotion.

There are basically four reasons people get angry. One is related to primal needs, such as food, shelter, and life. When these are threatened, a normal person feels vulnerable and responds with anger. If someone threatens one's life or family, the person needs to respond. This anger is not blameworthy. If humans were incapable of an angry response, we would have a society indifferent to crime and transgression. This would spell doom for human civilization. This is part of the wisdom behind the Qur'anic commandment to enjoin what is right and forbid what is evil.

The second reason is related to position, dignity, and protecting one's honor. Human beings are born with sensors that detect when others try to belittle them or when they are the object of contempt and scorn. The other side of this is when people view themselves with hubris and manufacture delusions of grandeur. They grow angry when they interpret normal and acceptable behavior towards them as beneath their dignity.

The third cause of anger is related to specific people and their particular sense of values. If, for example, a scholar sees that a book is being abused, he will become angry. An illiterate farmhand may not be vexed about the abuse of a book, though he may curse a man who breaks a pitchfork.

Finally, the fourth cause is *ghayrah*, commonly translated as jealousy. The Prophet ﷺ said that he himself had this type of protective jealousy: a sense of guarding what he held as dear. God has placed jealousy as part of human nature. For example, if men did not have jealousy about their wives, relationships would fall into dissolution. It is natural for a man to have this protective sense of jealousy regarding his wife, as long as it is not expressed in the form of oppressing her, which unfortunately happens frequently.

With regard to these causes of anger, Imam al-Ghazālī says that the first kind, which is related to material needs, is healthy as long as it is not taken to an extreme, such as a person stealing from others in order to secure food and shelter. The second kind, which is related to dignity, is also healthy, with the caveat of avoiding two extremes, haughtiness and abject humiliation. The Prophet ﷺ said, "The believer does not humiliate himself."

According to Sīdī Aḥmad Zarrūq, if ignorant people say something disparaging that does not relate to religion, then ignore it. One should not grow angry when there is no benefit in doing so. God, the Exalted, commanded the Prophet ﷺ when faced with the discourse of ignorant people, "*Be patient with what they say, then part from them graciously*" (QUR'AN, 73:10). The Prophet ﷺ praised a man named Abū Damdam who never became angry when people spoke ill of him, for when one speaks ill of another, the speaker not only acquires misdeeds, but his own good deeds transfer to the account of the victim.

Treatment

As for the spiritual disease of anger that consumes a person, Imam Mawlūd says there are two cures. One of them removes anger when it occurs, and the second suppresses or thwarts it. The first cure is to remember the extensive praise and goodness associated with forbearance and humility. Sīdī Aḥmad Zarrūq contends that the main reason people become angry is because they have inflated egos. For example, even though the Quraysh mocked the Prophet ﷺ, like children do, while persecuting him, the Prophet ﷺ did not become angry with them.

The ethic promoted here is to simply "let go" and not allow insult to penetrate and manipulate one's emotion. It is about maintaining control over one's own emotions, feeling secure. One should remember how much God, the Exalted, praises the qualities of humility and forbearance. One should race to attain the qualities and behaviors that the Best of those who praise, the Maker of the heavens and the earth, commends.

Humility and forbearance are praised in poetry and by all the different sages, even outside the religion of Islam. The Prophet ﷺ said that God elevates a person who is humble for the sake of God; but whoever tries to exalt himself, God debases him. The Prophet ﷺ was the most forbearing and forgiving of people. All the prophets were characterized by these qualities. None was known to be arrogant or easily angered.

Imam Mawlūd states next that one can control anger by recognizing that nothing takes place without God's leave: There is no power or might except with God. This life is a crucible of trial, and those who are heedless of this react severely when trials come upon them. The Prophet ﷺ said the strong man is not one who can wrestle people, but the man who controls himself when he is angry.

The Prophet ﷺ also advised that if one becomes angry, one should sit down. And if one is sitting, then one should recline. If neither of these helps, then one should perform the ritual ablution (*wuḍū'*) and then pray. The actual act of splashing water on the face can alter a person's mood. Anger often manifests itself in the face, which becomes red and warm. Once, when a person grew very angry before the Prophet ﷺ, he noticed how when one is extremely angry, one's face resembles Satan's. The Prophet ﷺ then said, "I have a word that, if spoken, will remove it from him. It is, 'I seek refuge in God from Satan, the accursed.'"

We know how anger can escalate. When conflict foments and becomes heated between two parties, they reflexively stand, which is the nature of rising tempers. It is important to make the parties sit, which lessens some of the anger. These simple remedies are not tricks; rather, they reveal how thin the veneer of anger can often be. Anger can be entirely irrational and require nothing more than a change of posture to reconstitute the mind. The Prophet's counsel is very telling of human nature; he reveals insights into the ebb and flow of human emotions and the ease with which we can alter our emotional condition. It is said that one of the ruses of Satan is to make what is easy appear difficult or even impossible; he whispers feelings of despair to make us grow despondent of God's mercy and thus surrender ourselves to the insidious view that we can never repent.

Anger sometimes arises between parents and their offspring, but this often can be avoided if parents treat their offspring appropriately in accordance to their ages. According to one Islamic model, the soul has three stages. In the first seven years, it is known as the appetitive soul. The primary concerns of children in this stage are eating and wanting attention. The second stage is the next seven years, the age of anger, when kids react strongly to stimuli and are annoyed easily.

The third is the rational stage, when reasoning and discernment reach their full capacity. ʿAlī ibn Abī Ṭālib encouraged parents to play with their children during the first stage, to indulge them, for they are discovering the world. They had been in a spiritual realm and have only recently entered the realm of the sensory. In the second stage, Imam ʿAlī counseled that parents should focus on training and discipline, for, in this stage, young people have a heightened capacity to receive and absorb information and thus learn new things. In the third stage, parents should befriend them and form a relationship that is amicable and full of kindness and companionship. After this, their children, now adults, should be set free.

Some people have a choleric temperament and hence a greater tendency to grow angry. ʿUmar ibn al-Khaṭṭāb, for example, was known to grow angry. But if we look further at him over the course of his development in Islam, his anger no longer got the best of him. In fact, it was the opposite. He tended to be forgiving and compassionate—especially near the end of his life. But he was also known for being a lion. Once the Prophet ﷺ was teaching a group of Qurayshī women. When they noticed that ʿUmar was coming, the women fled into another room. This was before the commandment for *ḥijāb* was revealed. ʿUmar came to the Prophet ﷺ and saw that he was amused. ʿUmar asked the Prophet ﷺ about what had amused him. The Prophet ﷺ said, "It is these Qurayshī women: when they see you, they flee." The Prophet ﷺ called back the women, whereupon ʿUmar asked them, "How is it that you flee from me and you are not shy in front of the Messenger of God? He is more worthy of your shyness!" And they said, "You are harsher than the Messenger of God. He does not become angry." And the Prophet ﷺ laughed and said, "If you, ʿUmar, went down one path, Satan would take another."

Heedlessness

POEM VERSES 138–140

Heedlessness is being careless concerning what God has commanded one to do and has prohibited.

Scholars of this science consider [heedlessness] to be the source of all wrongdoing. Its cure is to be found in four deeds, all of which possess rectifying qualities:

Seek forgiveness from God; visit the righteous; invoke benedictions upon the Prophet ﷺ; and recite [God's] Book.

Definition

Heedlessness (*ghaflah*) is a terrible lack of attention to what is infinitely more important in one's life than material goods. Heedlessness is a key concept often discussed in Islamic spiritual treatises and is referred to in many passages of the Qur'an. Imam al-Junayd, a prominent ninth century scholar, argues that heedlessness is the one pathogen that breeds all the rest of the diseases of the heart. The Arabic word for a simpleton is *mughaffal*, a person who is easily fooled. In our context, it is a person who is easily diverted from what is essential and consequential toward what is ephemeral and ultimately pointless.

According to some linguists, the Arabic word for "human being," *insān*, comes from the word *uns*, which refers to "intimacy," for the human being needs close companionship. Other linguists, however, believe it comes from the Arabic word *nasya*, which means to forget, implying that one of the characteristics of human beings is forgetfulness; this further implies that we need to be reminded often, which explains the centrality of repetition in spiritual practices.

The heedlessness that Imam Mawlūd speaks of here is that of its most menacing form: being heedless of divine purpose, accountability, the resurrection, ultimate standing, and judgment in the Hereafter. The full manifestation of these events is veiled to us by the thin wall of death, the timing of which is the secret that hovers above the heads of all men and women. Even though the reality of these things is hidden in the realm of the unseen, what is expected of us is to receive and accept the message the Prophet ﷺ brought.

This was the duty of all the prophets—to call people to believe in the unseen, to trust what they say, and to commit to their teachings. There is a well-known allegory of some people in a cave: at the entrance of the cave was a lamp which cast shadows that the people in the cave believed to be realities. When one person left the cave and saw the real world—the sun, the stars, and the trees—he raced back in the cave to tell the others that there was much more to their world than what they saw in their cave. But the people feared what he said, causing them to deny, ridicule, and then physically attack him. The prophets came to rouse people from their stupor, to take them from their delusion and heedlessness to awareness. Many of the prophets were slain; all faced harsh opposition.

In the Qur'an, you will find *ghaflah* mentioned several times in different forms, but almost invariably referring to unawareness. The Qur'an uses other words to refer to unawareness. Those who laugh at the Qur'an are *sāmidūn* (QUR'AN, 53:61); they are so immersed in amusement they are oblivious of reality. On the Day of Reckoning, the heedless will be driven to their chastisement and be told along the way, "*You were once heedless of this. Now We have removed your veil [ghiṭā'] from you, so your sight this day is sharp!*" (QUR'AN, 50:22). God speaks of the disbelievers impervious to the message of the prophets as having a cover (*ghishāwah*) over their eyes (QUR'AN, 2:7).

The ultimate trauma of heedlessness, then, is not seeing reality as it truly is. It is choosing a way of living that allows divine signs to be left unnoticed. The Prophet ﷺ supplicated that God, the Exalted, show him things in their reality, distinguished and clear: "Show me the truth as truth and give me the ability to follow it; and show me falsehood as falsehood and give me the ability to avoid it." Imam Mawlūd says *ghaflah* is also heedlessness of what God has commanded and what He has prohibited, or seeing the difference between the two as irrelevant.

One of the cures for heedlessness is keeping good and sincere company. It is recognized in virtually all traditions and cultures that the company one keeps has inroads to one's heart and morality. When surrounded by people who are sincere and trustworthy, one only benefits from them. Even when a person errs, good companions remind him and set him right.

Treatment

The cure is in four practices that possess authentic rectifying qualities. The first is repentance and seeking forgiveness. As a matter of regular worship, one should ask for forgiveness (*istighfār*) at least 70 or 100 times a day, according to the Prophetic practice, which was closely followed by our righteous forebears (*salaf*). This practice is connected to accounting for one's deeds. At the day's end, the merchant looks at his ledger to calculate his earnings, to see what "the scales say," so to speak. The moral scales are no less important, and each of us is a merchant with regard to what we lost or gained with respect to God's pleasure. When there is loss, which is a frequent occurrence, seeking God's forgiveness restores balance.

The second practice is visiting (*ziyārah*) righteous people, who enjoy rank with God, the Exalted. Classically, the ranking of humanity proceeds as follows, as evinced in the verse of the Qur'an, (4:69): prophets (*al-nabīyyīn*); truthful ones (*al-ṣiddīqīn*); martyrs (*al-shuhadā'*); and the righteous (*al-ṣāliḥīn*). The word *ṣāliḥ* conveys the notion of soundness of heart and excellent character. More specifically, it refers to one who gives God His due right by fulfilling His commandments and avoiding what He prohibited. This is *ḥaqq al-ʿibādah*, God's right to be worshipped, which include rites of worship as well as excellent behavior towards other people. Hence, a righteous person does not cheat or lie. He or she is the kind of person whom one should seek out as company. Scholars have always encouraged visiting righteous people as part of the protocol of the spiritual ascendancy. These people include the living as well as the dead. If one goes to Medina, it is recommended to visit the graves of the great Muslims and convey salutations of peace to them. The Prophet ﷺ visited the gravesites of his fallen Companions. During the early part of his message, he forbade the visiting of graves, but later on, the Prophet ﷺ encouraged it. In pre-Islamic times, visiting graves was a form of idolatry. When the young community was purged of that, the Prophet ﷺ abrogated the previous command.

Visiting graves is a poignant reminder of death and the Hereafter. It is an armament against heedlessness. There is a hadith in which the Prophet ﷺ passed by a grave and saw a woman there weeping. He said to her, "It is better to be patient." Not recognizing the Prophet ﷺ, she replied, "You haven't been afflicted as I have." The Prophet ﷺ then left her. When someone later told her that it was the Prophet ﷺ that she had spoken to, she went to him and explained that she did not realize to whom she was speaking. The Prophet ﷺ explained to her that true patience (*ṣabr*) is the patience shown when a trial first afflicts one. If one shows patience a year after losing someone dear, that is not the patience the Qur'an praises. Thus, visiting graves of righteous loved ones requires composure and self-control.

It is excellent to visit the righteous among us who are alive—those who are truly pious and knowledgeable. One cannot judge another person by title. In many Muslim countries now, men are presented with the title of "shaykh" as inherited from the father. As a result, there are people with that title who are ignorant. There are charlatans in this world, and none is more dangerous than a religious charlatan.

A learned man in Fez, Morocco, said, "God has made the ways of gaining lawful provision innumerable. Someone who uses religious pretension in order to profit is especially wicked." This is not to say that earning a living by teaching religion is wrong. According to the scholars, this is entirely permissible. Although the very early forebears of Islam objected to it, the later scholars changed that position. They recognized that earning a living through teaching the Qur'an, for example, was honorable, especially as the demand for religious instruction grew exponentially, and teachers, like anyone else, were in need of a livelihood. Imam Mālik was given a good sum of wealth, but he was also known to spend it freely for the benefit of the needy. He was knowledgeable as well as judicious and very generous with his wealth.

One must combine knowledge of the outward Islamic sciences with inward spiritual experience to be truly considered a teacher. Unfortunately in today's age, people often impose a chasm between inward and outward aspects of Islam, so two camps are postured against one another. The best example, though, is that of the Prophet ﷺ, who represents the most perfect balance of inward and outward excellence.

When visiting a righteous person, the discourse should be substantive and not one of idle talk. One should seek to benefit in gaining knowledge and in the supplication of the righteous person. In fact, one should ask for being continually remembered in their prayers, for their prayers might be more acceptable to God than one's own.

Just as one is recommended to visit the righteous, one should strive to be the righteous person that others seek out to visit. Imam Ibn ʿAṭā'allāh said, "If you do not believe that God can take you at this moment and make you one of His saintly believers (*awliyāh*), then you are ignorant of His power."

The third cure is to invoke benedictions on the Prophet ﷺ. This is, in fact, a command from God, the Exalted, Himself: "*O you who believe, invoke benedictions upon [the Prophet] and salutations of peace*" (QUR'AN, 33:56). The Companion, Ubayy ibn Kaʿb, once asked the Prophet ﷺ how much of his litany of remembering God (*dhikr*) should be benedictions on the Prophet ﷺ. He said that a fourth would be good, and "If you add more, it is better." Ubayy then asked, "And if I were to make it half?" The Prophet ﷺ said it was good, and "If you add more, it is better." Ubayy then asked, "And if I were to make it three–quarters?" The Prophet ﷺ said it was good, and "If you add more, it is better." Ubayy then declared that he would make all of his *dhikr* this way; the Prophet ﷺ said, "That is good." There is great light associated with invoking prayers of benediction upon the Prophet ﷺ. Sīdī Aḥmad Zarrūq once said, "If you do not have a *murabbī* [a spiritual mentor], then say prayers of blessings upon the Prophet ﷺ, which acts as a *murabbī*." Many scholars have attested to the fact that sending prayers of blessings upon the Prophet ﷺ purifies the soul. (Some recommend that one repeat it at least 500 times a day.) Some people make it their practice to repeat it 5,000 times a day. Imam Mālik constantly sent prayers of blessings on the Prophet ﷺ. The *muḥaddithūn* (scholars of prophetic traditions) are well known for this practice.

The fourth cure for heedlessness is the recitation of the Qur'an. Reciting it with *tadabbur* (reflection) awakens the heart. However, plain recitation is beneficial as well. Learned Muslims have recommended that a person recite one–thirtieth of the Qur'an (*juz*) every day. If this is difficult, then reciting Sura Yāsīn (36) after the dawn prayer, Sura al-Wāqiʿah (56) after the sunset prayer, and Sura al-Mulk (68) after the evening prayer greatly benefit the soul. (New Muslims should strive with their utmost to learn how to read the original Arabic text of the Qur'an. Meanwhile, one is advised to listen to the well-known Qur'an reciters on audio devices or read a good English translation until one is able to read the Arabic. It is important for one to be regularly engaged with the Book of God.) The actual sounds of the language of the Qur'an—the breathtaking rhythms and words—are a medicine. From the perspective of energy dynamics, every substance has a resonance at a specific wavelength. A medicine resonates in order to cure the disease. So, too, do the sounds of recitation of the Qur'an: "*O humankind, there has come to you from your Lord counsel and healing for what is in the breasts, and a guidance and a mercy to the believers*" (QUR'AN, 10:57). When one recites the Qur'an, one moves his or her tongue pronouncing revealed words of the Lord of the heavens and the earth. And these words have a powerful and unique sound. People are often amazed at the sound of the Qur'an when they hear it for the first time. The beauty of the Qur'an is in its meanings as well as the sound of its recitation.

These are the four cures that Imam Mawlūd offers for heedlessness. God warns the Prophet ﷺ from conforming to those whose hearts are in the state of heedlessness (QUR'AN, 18:28). God increases the heedlessness of people who turn away from the truth.

An interesting aspect of heedlessness is that everyone will eventually be cured of it, no matter what the extent of this disease. The challenge is to be cured in this life, the time when our obedience in the arena of tests and trials holds meaning. The moment a person dies, veils are lifted. Even the denizens of Hellfire will no longer live in the Hell of heedlessness. We were created to remember God, and if it takes the heat of Hell to remind some, then that is how it will be. We ask God to make us among those who remember Him in this life and among those who are saved in the Hereafter.

Rancor

POEM VERSES 141–144

Rancor—O you who seek its elucidation—
is when the heart is bound to treachery,

Betrayal, or some trickery. The knot binding it to the heart
is resentful malice.

Show kindness toward the object of your rancor, and you
will cause your enemies to despair. Keep also in mind the
forgiveness, as mentioned in the sound tradition,

Promised twice a week on Mondays and Thursdays.

Definition and Treatment

Ghill is a malady of the heart that is closely related to rancor, extreme anger, and malice. It comes from the same Arabic root from which the word *aghlāl* originates, which is used in the Qur'an to mean yokes around the neck (QUR'AN, 36:8), as if to say that rancor dwells in a heart bound to rancor and treachery. Rancor is a pungent emotion that is rooted in being extremely angry at a person to the point that one wishes harm to come to him. But the ultimate victim of rancor is its carrier. For this reason, believers pray, "Our Lord, forgive us and our brethren who came before us in faith, and do not place into our hearts rancor for those who believe! Our Lord, You are kind, compassionate" (QUR'AN, 59:10). One of the great blessings of Paradise is that God will completely remove any semblance of rancor from one's heart (QUR'AN, 7:43,15:47).

Imam Mawlūd says that if a person feels rancor toward a particular person, he should show that person goodwill. By nature, people are naturally inclined to love those who do good to them. And if one shows a person good, feelings of rancor will fall to the wayside. Satan rejoices when believers fight with one another and bear negative thoughts and feelings. There is an authentic hadith about Mondays and Thursdays being special days in which God forgives people. When the angels come to God and say that two believers are wrangling with one another, God, the Exalted, says, "Leave them until they set things aright between themselves." The implication is that if a person has rancor toward another believer, God shall not forgive that person until he forgives his brother, for rancor is a serious affliction that festers in one's heart and blocks good things from coming to one.

Boasting and Arrogance

POEM VERSES 145–149

Boasting is counted among these peculiarities. It is defined as your praising yourself for good qualities.

You should deem its vertiginous mountain as insignificant—by which I mean, of course, arrogance. [Do this] if you desire it to collapse to the ground.

Do that by knowing your Lord and knowing yourself, for whoever knows these two is humbled and feels insignificant.

The station of arrogance negates the station of gratitude, just as humility, by its nature, engenders gratitude.

Avoid and beware of humiliation and lowliness; in fact, display pride with the affluent and arrogant one.

Definition

Imam Mawlūd speaks next about *fakhr*, which is the loathsome practice of boasting. Exceptionally odious is the practice of bragging about what one has not done or exerted any effort toward, like bragging about one's ancestry and borrowing from some past nobility. Boasting is a problematic behavior that universally evokes objection and is considered a spiritual disease. No one likes a boaster, one who walks with a swank and swagger, and one who cannot be in the company of other people without speaking about himself or drawing attention to what he has done. God Himself reveals His dislike of bragging: "*God does not love the arrogant and boasting ones*" (QUR'AN, 31:18, 57:23). The pre-Islamic Arabs used to shout out, "I am the son of so and so!" claiming that their pedigree somehow sufficed as a mark of their status and privilege, an ethic that loomed large in their social structure. Mawlānā Rūmī composed the lines, "Be not content with stories of those who went before you. Go forth and create your own story." Strive to be among those whom others speak of with veneration.

Imam Mawlūd mentions the force behind the culture of boasting, namely, arrogance (*kibr*). "Deem that mountain insignificant," he says, "if you desire to sink it to the ground." The word for "arrogance" in Arabic stems from a root-word signifying "growth," either in mass or age. With arrogance, what is alluded to is glorification and aggrandizement of the self.

The most villainous beings in history were filled with arrogance and false pride: Satan, Pharaoh, the opponents of the Prophet ﷺ, and many nefarious tyrants since. The Prophet ﷺ warned against arrogance: "No one who has an atom's weight of arrogance in his heart will enter Paradise." God said, "*I will divert My signs from those who show arrogance without right*" (QUR'AN, 7:146). That is, God recompenses the arrogant ones by turning them away from understanding His Book, His prophets, and His signs placed all around them as well as within their own selves. God also says that He "*sets a seal upon the heart of every arrogant tyrant*" (QUR'AN, 40:35), and "*He does not love those who wax arrogant*" (QUR'AN, 16:23). One of the attributes of God, the Exalted, is that He is the Proud (al-Mutakabbir), an attribute that is reserved for Himself. It is not becoming for anyone to have any of it in his or her heart.

Justice follows every vice. When it comes to arrogance, its possessors will culminate in being the most abject people in the Hereafter; they will envy those whom they once thought to be beneath them in honor and status, those who were patient, grateful, and humble in this life. There are many passages of the Qur'an and hadith that support this.

There are different qualities and types of arrogance. The first type is when a person deems himself superior to others. Imam al-Ghazālī said, "People of knowledge are in greater danger of arrogance than anyone else"; this is because the knowledge they have attained may lead them to feelings of superiority.

The second type of arrogance is in displaying contempt and scorn towards others. Once a man saw an old woman calling to the Prophet ﷺ in a boisterous manner, yet the Prophet ﷺ stopped to speak with her, showing no sign of annoyance. When the man saw the Prophet's calm reaction, he said, "Muḥammad ﷺ is a man unlike the kings of other lands." It is a marvel how some people act arrogantly because of their perceived piety, while the Prophet ﷺ, "the best of creation," remained humble.

The third type of arrogance relates to lineage. In some cultures, if one is aware of his "high birth," he is obliged to behave nobly. The Arabs manifested this. If a man was born into a clan known for generosity, it was mandatory for him to be generous. One of the blights of many societies is racism: people feel and act superior simply because of their race. The Qur'an nullifies false claims of superiority and states that the only rank that matters relates to one's relationship with God: "*Indeed, the most honorable of you in the sight of God are the most God-fearing of you. Surely, God is all-knowing, all-aware*" (QUR'AN, 49:13).

Many people who have lineage traceable to the Prophet ﷺ and his family feel honored. While this indeed is an honor in itself, it is something to be venerated when one's actions are likewise honorable. It is said, "If your actions hold you back, your lineage will not speed you up." Imam al-Ḥaddād once said, "No person of any consequence should respect or praise an ignorant man, even if he is of noble birth and virtuous ancestry, for respecting and praising such a person in his presence may have an adverse effect on him. It may deceive him concerning God, render him neglectful of proper behavior, and distract him from gathering provision for the Hereafter."

Treatment

There are several cures for arrogance. First, we should remember our humble organic origins. As the Qur'an reminds us, every one of us is created from a drop of semen (QUR'AN, 75:37). One of the righteous forebears said, "A man carries feces between his two sides." What is the source of arrogance for beings who carry filth within ourselves? God says, "*Perished is man! How ungrateful he is! From what stuff did He create him? From a sperm drop He created him and proportioned him*" (QUR'AN, 80:16–19). God also says, "*Let man reflect from what he was created. He was created from an ejected fluid that issues from between the loins and the ribs*" (QUR'AN, 86:5–7). Furthermore, God says, "*Has there come over man a time when he was nothing remembered? We created man from sperm drop mixed in order to try him*" (QUR'AN, 76:1–2). These reminders should suppress any insurgence of arrogance and conceit.

Muslims should venerate religious heroes. In studying the personalities of the Companions of the Prophet ﷺ, one learns of incredibly great people who were extraordinarily humble. The illustrious repository of prophetic hadith, Abū Hurayrah ؓ, once sat in the company of another person; this man immediately moved his feet away from Abū Hurayrah ؓ out of respect for the august Companion of the Prophet ﷺ. Upon noticing that, Abū Hurayrah ؓ asked, "Why did you move your feet?" The man replied, "Out of deference to you." Abū Hurayrah ؓ responded, "For someone like me? I do not see anyone in this gathering worse than me."

A cousin of ʿAlī ibn Abī Ṭālib ؓ once asked him, "Who is better, you or Abū Bakr?" Imam ʿAlī ؓ answered, "Abū Bakr." And when asked the same question about ʿUmar ؓ, he answered, "ʿUmar." He then asked him, "What rank do you have?" Imam ʿAlī ؓ replied, "I am a Muslim among many." Unfortunately, nowadays, people who do not even come close to the stature, knowledge, wisdom, and piety of Imam ʿAlī ؓ, nonetheless are so easily offended when they perceive others have slighted them. Furthermore, acts we perceive as humble are often attempts at attaining the mere appearance of humility.

Ibn ʿAṭā'allāh said, "If you are aware of your humility, then you are arrogant." However, other scholars say, "If you are not like the real people, at least mimic them." It is better to simulate humility than to be an outright arrogant man. Imam al-Ghazālī says, "If one wishes to master calligraphy, then he must go to a master calligrapher and repeat what he does."

The fourth type of arrogance is that which is owing to beauty. The cure is to realize that beauty can be the most illusory of things. Social conditioning impacts our sense of beauty more than many would admit. However, regardless of this being ignored or not, one should ponder over why beauty could even be a cause of arrogance? That is, how can one have an obnoxious sense of superiority for something one had nothing to do with? First of all, God is the Fashioner; it is He who gives all things their shapes and forms. Secondly, beauty does not last; it wanes, as the pressures of age and stress wear down flesh, so what remains is what one should have focused on the first place: the content of one's character, personal beliefs, and one's deeds.

The fifth type of arrogance is that which stems from having wealth. The affluent are notorious for showing contempt for those of lesser means. This is not to say that all wealthy people exhibit this disease. There are generous men and women who recognize the source and responsibility of wealth. However, they tend to be the exception.

The sixth type of arrogance is based on physical strength. A very strong man once approached the Prophet ﷺ and challenged him to wrestle. The Prophet ﷺ agreed, and the Prophet ﷺ threw him down to the ground twice! The man was astounded and declared, "I've never been thrown to the ground." His arrogance had been rooted in his personal strength, which he thought none could match.

The seventh type of arrogance is due to possessing an abundance of something. An example of this is a teacher having many students and thus regarding himself as being better than the other teachers who have fewer students. The same is true with those who boast of having many friends, especially those in so-called high places.

The eighth type of arrogance is linked to having knowledge. This type of arrogance is particularly insidious, since knowledge is a greatly honorable matter. However, a knowledgeable person may become deluded into believing himself to be superior over others due to the veneration shown to him.

These various eight qualities may sow the seeds of arrogance. God created humanity and has bestowed human beings with more blessings than He has given the rest of His creation. However, blessings are coupled with responsibility. The intellectual and volitional capacities of humankind are great responsibilities. Ironically, it is these very capacities which have the potential of causing people to forget that every blessing we have is a gift from God and is something that we are responsible for. The Qur'an states, "*[God] has created death and life to test you as to which of you is best in deed*" (QUR'AN, 67:2); "*Have We not given [man] two eyes, a tongue, and two lips, and shown him the two highways [of good and evil]? Yet he does not attempt the steep road [of good]*" (QUR'AN, 90:8–11). The steep road here is spending on orphans, relieving the distressed, and all other good actions that are difficult for the arrogant ones, as they feel that their wealth, strength, and prestige are borne of their own devices. People rejected the Prophet's message not because they were not convinced. They knew that what the Prophet ﷺ brought was the truth from God Himself, but they rejected him out of arrogance.

Many find the Muslim prayer objectionable because of its postures of humility and awe before God. What they struggle with is not merely the postures but their aversion to submit to God, being His servant. People have difficulty with that, claiming that they are "free." Astonishingly, these same "free" people are in bondage to their whims and passions.

Imam Mawlūd says that the key to avoiding or removing this disease is to know yourself, your origins, and your ultimate return. The Prophet ﷺ said, "I am the best of the children of Adam and I am not boasting." His honor was entirely based on his servitude to God, the Exalted—not on wealth, lineage, power, or authority. Whoever is humbled for the sake of God, God elevates in rank. Haughtiness and gratitude cannot coexist in one vessel. God increases in goodness those who are grateful. The station of arrogance invites only humiliation.

Imam Mawlūd says humility, by nature, leads to gratitude, for when one is humble before God, the Exalted, only then does one see the vast mercy God bestows upon His creation, even upon liars and disbelievers.

Imam Mawlūd's conclusion to this discussion touches upon the Islamic ethic of moderation (*wasaṭiyyah*). While humility is a praiseworthy virtue, if it is carried out excessively, it results in abasement. According to some classical Christian theological paradigms, abasement is praised, but that is not the case in Islam. Imam Mawlūd calls excessive humiliation here *dhul*, and this word is not used in the same sense here in which he uses it at the beginning of his poem, where he speaks of *dhul* as humility required for proper courtesy with God. In this context here, he is referring to abject humiliation before people. It is similar to the abasement that God, the Exalted, afflicted upon past communities because of their flagrant rejection of God, derision of His apostles, and mockery of His laws. Abject humiliation is disapproved of, even in the face of tribulation. Those who face tests with dignity and patience are praised. A hadith states, "A believer never humiliates himself." Hence, humility is different from humiliation.

Having *dhul* with respect to God is different from *dhul* with respect to creation. Imam ʿAbd al-Qādir al-Jīlānī once said, "All the doors to God are crowded except for one: the door of humility and humbleness." Having humbleness is one of the secrets of success, though it is hard on the soul. It is said, "Among the most noble things of this world is a rich man who is humble."

Displeasure with Blame

POEM VERSES 150–154

Displeasure with blame is a well-known disease of the heart. Concern with people's opinions and desiring their praise and displeasure at their criticisms

Are a barrier from achieving the station of excellence in worship. Overcoming that barrier is through the realization

That there is no benefit or harm unless it comes from [God], the Possessor of all dominion, Exalted and Majestic is He.

Furthermore, what is prohibited from this disease is what leads to the prohibited, just as Imam al-Ghazālī has elaborated.

The perfection of sincerity is that you do not give notice to any praise or blame that emanates from people.

Discussion

The next disease is the displeasure with blame. Blame is not something that people naturally embrace. It runs against human nature to love it. However, the problem occurs when fear of blame is coupled with the urgent desire for praise and approval by others, which is often the case. Being concerned with "creation's opinion" places a barrier between a person and the station of iḥsān, excellence in worship. ("Creation's opinion" here in this context simply refers to "other people's opinions," as opposed to being concerned with God's pleasure.) This is considered a disease of the hearts, as it results in guiding one's actions in deference to the praise of people or in an attempt to avoid their blame or disapproval, irrespective of the integrity and soundness of one's actions.

The Companions of the Prophet ﷺ exemplified complete loyalty to the ethics of Islam. Many times they were confronted with having to make decisions that would evoke displeasure among the people and tribes around Medina, but, nevertheless, the decisions they chose to make were in accordance to the teachings of the Prophet ﷺ. The more that one worries about how one's decisions will be received by people, the thicker the veil becomes with regard to God and His guidance.

Muslims have a great responsibility. God says, "*Thus have We made you a middle nation, so that you may be witnesses for humankind*" (QUR'AN, 2:143); hence, the Muslims comprise a people who should enjoin justice and remind humanity of God's rights. When people give up enjoining what is right or even admitting that there are absolute and objective values, which are not subject to the whims of mankind, then evil spreads. The best of witnesses was the Prophet ﷺ, then his Companions, and then their Successors. Each generation subsequently takes on this office of witnessing, although hardly to the degree exhibited in the early generations. Towards the end of earthly time, the world will be virtually without witnesses to truth, and truth itself will be scarce. No one will defend it. According to Imam al-Biqāʿī, one of the signs of the end of time is the handing over of the world to the disbelievers, with Muslims abandoning Islam and its claim upon Muslims to defend the truth and censure what is wrong. Sīdī Aḥmad Zarrūq said that the truth has the power to penetrate the hearts of people, including those whose hearts have a seal. Humanity has the right to have among us witnesses to the truth, those who are willing to defend the truth no matter how unpopular it may be.

According to Imam Mawlūd, overcoming the fear of blame is achieved through realizing that there is no benefit or harm except by God's permission and plan. This should sound familiar, as it is the recommended cure for many of the diseases discussed so far. Two of God's most excellent names are the Giver of benefit (al-Nāfiʿ) and the Bringer of harm (al-Ḍārr). These attributes are specific to God alone; no one else possesses them in the least. It is only God who can benefit, and only He who can permit harm. If a person is worried about how others receive him, then he is not aligned with reality.

According to a hadith, the Prophet ﷺ said to Ibn ʿAbbās,

> Be mindful of God, and God will protect you. Be mindful of God, and you will find Him in front of you. If you ask, ask of God. If you seek help, seek help from God. Know that if the whole nation were to gather together to benefit you with anything, it would benefit you only with something that God had already prescribed for you. And if [the whole nation] were to gather together to harm you, it would harm you only with something that God had already prescribed for you. The pens have been lifted and the ink has dried.

This does not mean that one should be reckless with his or her safety, nor does it mean that one should not take precautions. In the Battle of Uḥud, the Prophet ﷺ wore two coats of chainmail, and no one knew more of God's power and authority than he. Having awareness of God's attributes does not imply that people should stop using their intellects, for we live in a world of causes. There is room for diplomacy and discretion, particularly of knowing when it is best to say the truth. This discretion, however, is not informed by the fear of blame but rather by clarity regarding one's objectives. Having wisdom is completely different from seeking the approbation of others. The Prophet ﷺ said that the highest form of struggle (*jihād*) is to speak the truth in the face of a tyrant.

Imam Mawlūd says that the inordinate fear of blame can lead a person to engage in prohibited matters or to neglect obligations. If one worries about how people will receive him when he practices his faith, this can prevent him from performing obligations. The fear of blame interferes with faith. Deeds that are done for the sake of God cannot share other intentions, namely, pleasing people or seeking their favor. Doing something for the sake of God is the manifestation of strong faith. Whether one receives praise or not from anyone should be entirely inconsequential.

Antipathy Toward Death

POEM VERSES 155–163

Antipathy towards death is when one flees from it and becomes annoyed when it is even mentioned—

As if he is completely ignorant of [God's statement that] each soul shall taste death.

This is reckoned to be among the diseases of the heart. So be content with what God, the Exalted, has decreed.

But if one detests [death] not for its own sake, nor for the loss of pleasures that it entails,

But rather out of fear of being cut off from preparing for the Day of Judgment by obeying God more, [then it is not blameworthy].

Also, if one completely entrusts his affair to his Master, whatever He wills, either causing him to drop dead or giving him respite, it contents him.

Both of these attitudes towards death are commendable and praiseworthy. [Either way], disliking the reality of death in no way distances you from its proximity.

The one who constantly remembers death is ennobled with contentment, with his heart's activities directed toward obedience,

And with prompt repentance [when wrongs occur]. The one who is heedless of death is afflicted with the opposite of all three.

Definition and Treatment

Antipathy towards death is considered a disease of the heart. It refers to strong aversion to death to the point that its mere mention causes consternation. Such a person, Imam Mawlūd says, is in denial of the reality. God says, "*Every soul shall taste death*" (QUR'AN, 3:185); "*Say, the death from which you flee will overtake you. Thereafter, you will return to the Knower of the seen and unseen. He will then inform you of all that you had been doing*" (QUR'AN, 62:8). None of this suggests that one should leap into the throes of death. It merely disparages the ethic of chasing after the fleeting things of this world while rebuffing the imminence of death and what comes thereafter. Nowadays, death is usually considered a morbid topic that is uncouth to discuss. And when it is discussed, it is often turned into some deadline before which people are supposed to squeeze in all their life's pleasures. The Muslim's view should be completely different. To speak about death is to speak about life and the urgency to live a faithful and wholesome life before death overtakes us.

Shaykh Ibn al-Ḥabīb said, "In death there are a thousand reposes for the Muslim. As long as you are in this world, there is not a cell in your body that does not experience pain and disease. Once you are out of this world, all of that ends." For the believer, there is comfort in death, for the believer is taken from an abode of difficulty and trial to one of peace and unfathomable freedom. In Islam, the mourning period is short and should not be prolonged. The irony of extending the mourning period is that doing so is rooted in excessive love of *dunyā* (the world). The more one covets this world, the greater the sense of loss when a loved one dies.

Everyone experiences the loss of a loved one. When the Prophet ﷺ lost his son Ibrāhīm, he wept but also praised God, the source of life and death. People who have strong faith in God and in the afterlife tend to handle death well and also handle calamities and tribulations well. Maurice Bucaille, the well-known French physician, said that what attracted his interest in Islam was how North Africans in France faced death. As a physician exposed to disease and death, he observed many of his own countrymen not knowing how to die or to handle death.

The fear of death is natural. One reflexively protects himself from it. When angels in the form of human beings visited Prophet Abraham ﷷ, he offered them food. When he saw that they did not reach for the food, he grew fearful. Scholars say that Abraham ﷷ thought they had come to take his life. The Prophet ﷺ encouraged believers to desire a long life for two reasons: to make up for past iniquities or to increase good deeds.

The one who remembers death is ennobled by certain characteristics, which include contentment and a lack of covetousness. The Prophet ﷺ said, "Contentment is a treasure that is never exhausted." He also prayed, "O God, provide for my family with what suffices them, and grant them contentment with it." The wealthy soul is one that is content. This contentment is not the kind that originates from stupidity or not knowing any better. It is contentment that is informed by knowledge and by reflection on death and its meaning.

Second, the remembrance of death gives one energy to achieve good deeds: "*Wealth and sons are the ornaments of the life of this world, while enduring righteous deeds are better with your Lord in reward and better in hope*" (QUR'AN, 18:46).

Third, remembrance of death engenders seeking repentance when one slips or errs. Penitence rectifies wrong action, and that is the gift of remembering death. When one lives with this realization, he or she becomes prompt in seeking God's forgiveness. Those who are heedless of death often have no compunction in doing wrong, since death is not a factor in their lives. They often carelessly view the Day of Judgment as some distant event hardly worth worrying about or some ancient notion formed in a primordial epoch of human development.

Obliviousness to Blessings

POEM VERSES 164 166

Among the faults of the soul is obliviousness to blessings.
Its root lies in inattentiveness to [the statement],

"*Whatever blessings you have* [are from God]." By simply remembering this and keeping in mind other verses of admonition, such as,

He does not change..., and *If you show gratitude...*, then this chronic disease can be excised from you.

Definition and Treatment

The next disease is oblivion of blessings, a lack of understanding and acknowledgement, and noxious disregard that "*whatever blessings you have are from God*" (QUR'AN, 16:53). The blessings that come to us, night and day, are beyond numeration, as the Qur'an reminds. These blessings come in all forms—what we can see and touch (by way of material goods: food, clothing, shelter, wealth, and the like), as well as what we cannot see (such as safety, friendship, love, health, and protection from harm and calamity).

The Qur'an begins with the phrase translated as, "*In the name of God, the Merciful, the Mercy-Giving*" (QUR'AN, 1:1). According to some scholars, "Merciful" (*raḥmān*) refers to the Giver of the major blessings, while "Mercy-Giving" (*raḥīm*) implies the Giver of subtle blessings, which are not perceived until they are removed. For example, we blink thousands of times in a day without thought. There are people, however, who require artificial lubrication because their tear glands do not function. There are countless blessings related to the eye, let alone other aspects of our lives, such as our ability to walk in balance without needing to consciously stimulate dozens of muscles required to take one step. Our thumbs permit us to do with our hands what most creatures cannot attempt. God has made food delicious and flavorful instead of bland. He has also given us dignity in our nutrition, which is a tremendous blessing, especially when one considers the way carnivores devour their prey.

While we cannot count our blessings, we are commanded to be grateful for them:

So let man reflect on the food he eats. Indeed, We have poured down water in showers. Then We split the land in clefts. Then We caused to grow grain therein, and grapes and fresh herbage, and olives trees and date palms, and dense orchards and fruits and pasture—all provision for you and for your cattle (QUR'AN, 80:24–32).

The fact that the Qur'an has been revealed to tell us to reflect on these blessings is in itself a great blessing, for, without guidance, the human being cannot on his own determine out how to live. To deny God's blessings can lead to outright disbelief and denial of God, the Exalted.

"*God never changes any blessing He has bestowed upon a people until they first change what is in themselves*" (QUR'AN, 8:53). God will not take away a blessing unless people show ingratitude. A poet said, "If you have a blessing, guard it, for disobedience shall snatch it away." Gratitude to God protects one from having blessings removed.

Istidrāj is God's allowing an ingrate to flaunt his blessings and not diminishing the ingrate's blessings in the least. In fact, God may even increase that blessing. The ingrate is then deluded into thinking that God really loves him or her, and the only thing worse than a misguided person is the person who is astray but believes himself to be favored by God. "*As for man, whenever his Lord tries him by honoring him and bestowing favors on him, he says, 'My Lord has honored me.' And whenever He tries him by restricting his provision, he says, 'My Lord has humiliated me'*" (QUR'AN, 89:15–16). Qur'anic commentators say that this passage shows the confusion of people in the way they interpret the blessings they receive. When they are the recipients of great wealth, they see themselves as especially pleasing to God. And when their provision is restricted, they feel God is debasing them. However, people often miss the reality that wealth is a test from God to see if its recipient will be generous or miserly. The same applies when wealth is restricted: Will a person be patient and content or feel despair and bitterness?

Certain qualities benefit a person in the short and long term, such as knowledge and excellent character. Similarly, certain characteristics harm a person immediately and in the long run, such as ignorance and obnoxiousness. Furthermore, some actions offer immediate gratification, but the long-term benefits are nil. Carnal desires (*shahawāt*) are generally of this type. If a person overeats, he experiences immediate gratification; but in the long-term, doing so invites health problems. Also, other actions may be beneficial in the long-term but somewhat uncomfortable in the short. For example, one may find it difficult to stop eating to his full, but the long-term benefits are obvious. This is also true with sexual intimacy: being patient until marriage may be uncomfortable and even frustrating, but its benefit is far greater than any temporary pleasure attained in falling into sin.

Those who are ignorant see only short-term relief as a blessing and disregard the benefits of patience and temporary discomfort. On the other hand, knowledge opens the eyes to the long-term benefits, which last forever. In a study conducted on some children, researchers left cookies out on a table and told the children that they can have either one cookie now or two later. Consistently, the children who scored better on intelligence tests waited for the two–cookies option rather than indulging in one cookie right away. After following these children for thirty years, it was found that those who opted for the long-term gain were better adjusted, better educated, and more successful in their marriages.

Intelligence is linked to morality, as to be moral one must be willing to put off a short-term gain for a long-term benefit that ultimately is greater and everlasting. This kind of intelligence is conditioned by Islam. Sayyidunā ʿUmar ﵁ said, "We are a people to whom God has given dignity with Islam; but if we seek dignity elsewhere, God will humiliate us."

Blessings are either roots or branches. Roots include faith, Islam, health, safety, and wellbeing. The branches are money, clothing, shelter, and the like. According to the Qur'an, the Children of Israel disputed with a prophet among them over the choice of Saul (Ṭālūt) as their king because he was not a man of great wealth. However, their prophet told them that God has given Saul knowledge and strength (QUR'AN, 2:247), which are blessings greater than wealth.

The Prophet ﷺ once asked a man, "Do you know what the completion of a blessing is?" The Prophet ﷺ told him, "Entering Paradise." The best of blessings are those connected with entering Paradise. Faith, patience, good character, swiftness in doing good, and promptness in worship are blessings from God, and they are everlasting. Islam itself is the completion of God's blessings upon humanity: "*This day, I have perfected for you your religion, and I have completed My blessings upon you, and I have chosen Islam for you as your religion*" (QUR'AN, 5:3).

The ornaments of this life include houses, furnishings, clothing, and the like. The more one acquires of these blessings, the more he will be accountable for. The Prophet ﷺ said that the meat, dates, and cool water that we consume are of those things we will be asked about, even the sandals on our feet.

To be *zāhid* (ascetic) does not always mean a lack of material possession. There is asceticism of the heart, in which one is not attached to the material world and is indifferent to it. In other words, a person's character and level of faith will not change if he loses his wealth. That is the sign of a *zāhid*. However, if one falls apart and plunges into despondency when losing something valuable, it shows an inordinate attachment to worldly life.

Derision

POEM VERSES 167–169

As for derision, tend to it with the same treatment used for arrogance, and with the knowledge that one's purpose in [derision] is to humiliate someone.

Yet by doing that, a person actually humiliates himself with God and is recompensed with misfortune.

Also, treat it by knowing the severe warning that has come in Ṣaḥīḥ Muslim about showing contempt for any Muslim.

Definition and Treatment

The next disease is derision, ridiculing people, making jest at their expense. Moses ﷺ told his people that God had commanded them to sacrifice a cow. They replied, "Are you mocking us?" Moses ﷺ then told them, "*I seek refuge in God from being ignorant*" (QUR'AN, 2:67). Hence, mocking people is a form of ignorance, whether it is lampooning, caricaturing, or name-calling. Humor and levity are important in human life. But levity as a way of life harms the spiritual heart. Furthermore, laughter and amusement at the expense of the dignity of others is wholly inappropriate, although it is the staple of the comedians of our day.

Imam Mawlūd says that the cure for the psychology and practice of mockery is similar to that of arrogance, since a person who mocks another most likely sees himself as superior to his victim. ʿAlī ibn Abī Ṭālib said, "Do not belittle anyone, for he may be a saint of God." Even if one sees a man inebriated and bellicose, vomiting in the street, one should not ridicule him, for one does not know what his future holds. Imam al-Qurṭubī said, "When he was bowing down to idols in Mecca,

ʿUmar ibn al-Khaṭṭāb was still beloved to God." Only God knows the seal of people and their destinies. A Moroccan proverb says, "Never mock any creature of God, for it might be beloved to He who created it." The Qur'an says,

O you who believe, do not let people mock another people; for it may be that these are better than them; nor should women mock other women, for it may be that these are better than them. And do not taunt one another nor insult each other with nicknames (QUR'AN, 49:11).

God also commanded, "*Do not revile those who call upon others apart from God, for they may then revile God out of ignorance*" (QUR'AN, 6:108). This Qur'anic ethic guards against inciting people to do things that are sacrilegious and harmful to their own souls, for if people start to curse God, the Exalted, they invite the worse kind of harm. Even in the context of triumph, being boastful and exulting is ignoble. The Prophet ﷺ was never boastful when victorious. He was completely magnanimous and grateful to God, the Exalted. When he entered Mecca, his beloved city, during the final conquest, he entered it with his head bowed and granted clemency to its inhabitants even though they had tortured, mocked, and reviled him. He exemplified complete beauty in character rooted in compassion and mercy.

Supplicating God against one's enemies is not forbidden; in fact, it is recommended that people ask for victory when being attacked or occupied. For example, the situation in occupied Palestine is extremely difficult and unjust. It is the Palestinians' right to ask God to relieve them of the tyranny from which they suffer. However, it also important not to generalize and associate those who are peaceful with the true aggressors. The Prophet ﷺ spoke well of the Jews, Mukhayraq and Rifāʿah, and his own wife Ṣafiyyah had Jewish relatives that she continued to visit on Sabbath. The idea that all Jews are evil is as absurd as the idea that all Muslims are terrorists. In our interdependent and pluralistic world, avoiding the pre-modern attitudes that set groups against one another has never been more important. Many Jewish thinkers have condemned the occupation and are among the most vociferous critics of Israeli injustice. An example of an excellent prayer to make when oppressed or occupied is *al-Duʿā' al-Nāṣirī* which was written by a Moroccan scholar. In fact, many Moroccans believe that Morocco was freed from the French because that particular prayer was read nationwide during the French occupation.

People can be transformed. The opponents of the Prophet ﷺ were particularly vicious against Muslims. Hind actually bit into the liver of the Prophet's uncle, Ḥamzah, when he was martyred at the Battle of Uḥud. However, she later became Muslim, and hence became a Companion of the Prophet ﷺ, a member of that special generation of humanity. In fact, she even narrated hadith that can be found in the well-known compilations. Repentance is a recourse that the Lord of the Worlds has given humanity. Reflecting on the ethic that the Qur'an communicates to us in the aforementioned passages reveals that there is strength in dealing nobly with people. It is simply a better way to live. The treatment for derision is to realize that the essence of mockery is to humiliate people. Those who mock people in this life shall be mocked in the Hereafter, for it is a divine law that God recompenses people with the like of what they have done.

Comprehensive Treatment for the Heart

POEM VERSES 170–175

A comprehensive treatment plan for the heart's diseases
is to deny the self of its desires,

Enjoin hunger, keep worship vigilance in the night,
be silent, and meditate in private;

Also keep company with good people who possess
sincerity, those who are emulated in their states and statements;

And, finally, take refuge in the One unto whom all affairs
return. That is the most beneficial treatment for all of the
previous diseases.

This must be to the point in which you are like a man
drowning or someone lost in a barren desert and see no
source of succor

Except from the Guardian, possessor of the greatest power.
He is the One who responds to the call of the distressed.

Discussion

Imam Mawlūd's approach in offering the cures for these diseases is like the story of the Gordian Knot of the kingdom of Phrygia, whose king offered his dominion to whoever was able to unravel the knot. Many tried and failed. When Alexander the Great was shown the knot, he pulled out his sword and cut through it. Diseases of the heart are like the Gordian Knot, and the best way to treat them is to cut through them. Imam Mawlūd completes his discussion on the various diseases and turns his attention to a comprehensive treatment plan for the heart, which focuses on curbing the soul from its own excessive desires. To accomplish this, he states that one must engage in hunger, vigilance during the nights, silence, and meditation in private. The Prophet ﷺ said, "None of you [fully] believes until his desires are in accordance with what I have brought." Hence, one's faith is not complete until his desires do not conflict with the message the Prophet ﷺ was given. The way to achieve this alignment is to prohibit the soul of all things that are not in accordance with Islam, whether its law or its spirit. One should persist in this until the desire is tamed and compliant with divine dictates: "*As for he who transgresses and prefers the life of this world, Hell is [his] abode. And as for he who fears standing before his Lord and refrains his soul from passions, Paradise is [his] abode*" (QUR'AN, 79:37–41). Severing the bonds of slavery to the whims of the soul leads to happiness.

A typical bookstore usually carries several books that deal with people's addictions and their inability to control themselves. This publishing phenomenon is a response to social realities. For Muslims, it is prayer that teaches one how to become disciplined with one's hours and days. Islam offers cleanliness through ablution and a consciousness of the passing of hours. Fasting is a universe in itself, a realm in which one learns about discipline in the most direct way with regard to the tongue, stomach, genitals, and eyes. Islam places great emphasis on discipline because there is so much at stake. Without discipline, religion is impossible.

According to Christian tradition, the seven deadly sins comprise arrogance, anger, envy, sloth, greed, gluttony, and lust. The last two relate to one's base desires, and they are the chief desires of the soul. Gluttony and lust are founded upon natural inclinations of hunger and sexual attraction. The pathology related to them, however, pertains to excessiveness therein and satisfying one's urges in a forbidden manner. Imam al-Ghazālī dealt with these impulses at great length in a section of his *Iḥyā' ʿUlūm al-Dīn*, which has been translated masterfully by T. J. Winter: *Breaking the Two Desires* (Cambridge: Islamic Texts Society, 1995).

The stomach is the source of one's primary impulse. If one can learn to control the desire for food, other issues of disciplines begin to fall into place as well, for gluttony is the fuel for lust, and fasting breaks gluttony. The Prophet ﷺ advised that unmarried people fast frequently in order to keep their sexual desires in check. Imam al-Qushayrī said, "For me to raise my hand from my plate while I am still hungry is better than the whole night in prayer."

Spiritual masters traditionally have focused on hunger. The goal is not to create a nation of anorexics but to cut the knot that binds self-discipline. We do things often out of blind conditioning. When it comes to food, many have been drilled into believing that three meals are not only normal, but necessary for proper nutritional fulfillment. However, this is not true. The caloric intake of an average American far exceeds what is needed for physiological wellbeing. As a result, America is now recognized as the most obese nation on earth, according to the National Institutes of Health (NIH).

Once the Prophet ﷺ served a bowl of milk to a guest from Yemen who was not Muslim. When the man finished drinking, the Prophet ﷺ asked if he wanted more, and the man said he would. This continued until the guest drank seven bowls of milk, which was far more than what he needed. However, this man later became Muslim, and the Companions noticed that thereafter he drank only one bowl of milk. The Prophet ﷺ told them, "The disbeliever eats with seven intestines, while the believer eats with one."

People nowadays consume much more food than ever before, and this is especially the case with meat. In the past, meat was eaten infrequently even by the affluent, who had it once or twice a week. The poor ate meat once or twice a year, mainly around the time of Eid. Furthermore, snacking has become so common now that many do not go for more than a few hours without consuming something. Convenience stores and vending machines are found everywhere. This abundance was unheard of not long ago. All of this has virtually turned people into grazing animals, which is an anathema to spiritual wellness.

In their study of eating habits, sociologists have found that the average American has twenty food contacts a day. In most traditional cultures, meals were set for specific times, and eating between meals was not acceptable. Nowadays, for many, having a meal has been dispossessed of formality. Within the family, it no longer serves a social purpose for many. Family members can reside in the same home yet live virtually apart from one another so that there is barely any interaction between parents and children and among siblings and any other relatives. There is now a much more callous relationship between human beings and their meals, a disconnection from the source of their nutrition and insensitivity to the flesh they eat.

The combination of overeating and breakdown of table manners impairs one's ability to build fortitude. A Muslim should begin each meal, saying, "In the name of God." The purpose of this, besides sanctifying a mundane act, is to consciously remember the source of the provision, one's Lord. Instead of eating alone, one should attempt to find company to share the meal with. When the meal is complete, one should praise God. If one is hosted, one should thank the hosts and pray for them.

Ramadan is a time to experience hunger with good cheer and renewed gratitude, a time to divorce oneself from the world and be reminded of one's spiritual soul. However, one can rob Ramadan of an important benefit by overeating at night in order to make up for what was missed during the day. The nights can become lengthy buffets and worship vigils become secondary (or ignored).

People who have a problem with excessive eating should start at least by lessening the portion of what they normally eat, which is the beginning of discipline. It is also advised to eat with other people, for eating with guests would make a person more conscious of being a glutton. Also, the more people who sit around a table, the greater the blessings (*barakah*). Finally, one should decrease the number of meals in a day.

It is not surprising that Imam Mawlūd mentions hunger first among the comprehensive treatments for the heart. Eating is one of the most abused behaviors. We are conditioned to think that hunger is sated only when we feel full. One typical meal served in an average American restaurant can feed a family in West Africa.

Imam Mawlūd mentions next the night prayer vigil. If one wishes to enliven the heart, then one should give it time with its Lord in the stillness of the dark, even if it is only two *rakʿahs*. Imam Mālik says to never leave the night prayer vigil even for a little time. Being consistent with the night prayer (and all other meritorious things) is important. It is better to rise at night for just ten minutes on a regular basis than to stay up for hours one night and then sleep the next night. The performance of this prayer on a patchwork basis results in little benefit. Sīdī Aḥmad Zarrūq said it is like "drilling here and there, never finding water anywhere."

The Prophet ﷺ said, "Spread peace, feed needy people, and pray at night when others are asleep, and you will enter Paradise with ease." In the Qur'an, the Prophet's Night Prayer is associated with the elevated rank he shall be granted by God: "*And in a portion of the night, rise therein for Night Prayer—an extra act of devotion for you. It may be that your Lord shall raise you to a praiseworthy station*" (QUR'AN, 17:79). God, the Exalted, commends those who deprive their sides from their beds, resist sleep (which the body loves), and rise for prayer (QUR'AN, 32:16).

It is not our tradition for one to be excessive in spiritual practices, such that one is deprived of sleep to the point of becoming psychotic or deprived of food to the point that one's health is damaged. On the contrary, one should learn to control the soul's desires and not be controlled by them. The Prophet ﷺ said that our bodies have rights over us: they are food, drink, and companionship.

Not all of the Companions performed the night prayer, but many did. For us, what is rational and reasonable is to have some steady practice. It is good to start with short suras of the Qur'an during the prayer. If one makes a habit of spending a portion of the night in prayer and happens to oversleep until the time of dawn prayer, then it is permissible to perform the night prayer vigil before the dawn prayer, as long as one has enough time to pray the dawn prayer comfortably. This is a valid opinion.

There is a hadith in which the Prophet ﷺ said about ʿAbd Allāh ibn ʿUmar that he was an excellent man, "but if only he were to spend time in night prayer." Scholars take from this hadith that a person can be excellent even if he does not practice the night prayer, but that an excellent person would be exceptional if he or she prayed it. When ʿAbd Allāh ibn ʿUmar heard the Prophet's ﷺ statement, he never once deserted the night prayer (*qiyām*). Also there is the famous hadith of ʿĀ'ishah who said that the Prophet ﷺ used to stand in prayer for so long that his feet would swell. She said to him, "O Messenger of God, why pray so long when God has forgiven everything you have done in the past and the future?" The Prophet ﷺ said, "Should I not be a grateful servant?"

Scholars say that anytime after evening prayers (*ʿishā'*) is considered time for the night prayer vigil (*qiyām*). Some say, however, that one should actually sleep then get up, while others say that sleep is not a requirement. People differ in what they are capable of doing. For physiological reasons, some have an especially difficult time waking up for *qiyām*. For them, perhaps, it is better to pray *qiyām* before they sleep. For other people, it is easy to rise an hour or two before dawn. Right before dawn, sleep is the heaviest. Imam Ibn ʿAṭā'allāh said there is great wisdom that God, the Exalted, obliges us to rouse ourselves from sleep when it is most difficult: mind over matter. The self-discipline gained from this practice is very important to us.

In an attempt to keep a worshipper in slumber, Satan ties three heavy knots on one's head. The Prophet ﷺ said that when one wakes up and says the supplication for awakening, "Praise be to God who has restored life to me after He has taken my soul, and to Him is the resurrection," one knot is undone. When one makes ablution, the second knot is undone. And when one performs the prayer, the third knot is undone.

The Prophet ﷺ often recited the closing verses of the third sura of the Qur'an (Āl ʿImrān) and was very moved by them. The Prophet's Companion, Bilāl, came to the Prophet's home to announce the coming of prayer. Bilāl saw that the Prophet ﷺ had been weeping and asked him, "You weep while God has forgiven you for all of your past and your future?" The Prophet ﷺ said to him, "O Bilāl! Shall I not be a grateful servant while God has revealed to me this night verses [of the Qur'an]," that is, the closing verses of Āl ʿImrān (3:190–200). "Woe to him who reads these verses and does not ponder them!"

The night prayer vigil, like other acts of worship, is a gift that can be taken away when, for example, the worshipper starts to backbite, gossip, slander, consume unlawful food, earn illicit wealth, and so on. One who has established an excellent regimen of worship may suddenly find oneself unable to continue. It may be that the blessing of being able to perform this righteous practice is removed because of something bad one had done. When this occurs, one should repent and strive to restore the practice. A scholar said, "I once said something about someone I should not have said, and I was deprived of the night prayer for forty days." A man said that at the end of his life he went bankrupt because decades before he called out to a man, "*Yā muflis*" or "O bankrupt one!"

It is recommended that the last prayer be the *witr* prayer (the final prayer of the evening). It is also preferred that the *witr* prayer be performed immediately before dawn breaks. This requires that a person get up for night prayer. But if a person does not have a night prayer regimen, then it is acceptable to pray the *witr* before sleeping.

Shaykh al-Ḥabīb said, "Take the path of ease with yourself in order for you to progress in your yearnings." One should not push oneself to the point that supererogatory vigils are a chore instead of a delight. He then said, "A prayer performed with love is better than a thousand devoid of it." Moderation ensures consistency and, as a result, the reaching of one's destination.

Imam Mawlūd mentions next the importance of silence. The Prophet ﷺ said, "If a person is given silence, he is given wisdom." The tongue is a great temptation. It is easy to say something that brings ruin upon its speaker. Learning how to control the tongue is an enormous discipline. Imam al-Shāfiʿī said that whenever he was in a gathering and wanted to say something, he would check his soul and be sure that his intentions were pure and were not to prove himself or flaunt his knowledge. Imam al-Shāfiʿī was a man of great intelligence and encyclopedic knowledge, yet he often enjoined silence upon himself. He once said, "I never had a debate with anyone except that I prayed to God that He make the truth appear on the tongue of my opponent so I could submit to it."

When the Prophet ﷺ spoke, he always said the truth, even in levity. He disliked verbosity and cautioned his Companions about the tongue and what it earns. If it is words for the sake of words, it is a waste of time and a sign of bad character. Imam Mālik said about one of his students, "He is a good man except he speaks a month's worth of words in a day."

Imam Mawlūd mentions spiritual isolation for the purpose of reflection. Some remember death through visualization, using the puissance of imagination for visualizing their bodies washed, wrapped, and lowered in the grave. Others reflect on the attributes of God, the Exalted, by methodically pondering the meanings of each of His divine names that speak of God's awesome power, knowledge, clemency, mercy, creative powers, and more.

Next in the overall treatment of the heart, Imam Mawlūd speaks of the importance of keeping the company of good people, which is God's command: "*O you who believe, fear God and be among the truthful ones*" (QUR'AN, 9:119). It is astonishing how people can influence others simply by being in each other's company. Imam al-Ḥaddād said, "The company one keeps has major effects. It may lead to either benefit and improvement or harm and corruption, depending on whether the company is that of pure and eminent people or those who are immoral and evil. This effect does not appear suddenly but is a gradual process that unfolds with time."

Imam Ibn ʿAṭā'allāh said, "Do not take as a companion someone whose state will not elevate you and whose speech does not direct you to God." In the same vein, Sīdī Aḥmad Zarrūq said that one should befriend people who elevate one's station. Good company includes those who are in the state of gratitude; they are thankful for what they have and do not waste time complaining. One takes on their excellent characteristics. Sīdī Abū al-Ḥasan said, "Anyone who tells you to indulge in the world is defrauding you." Shaykh Ould al-Khadīm says that when it comes to worldly possessions, it is good to associate with people who have lesser means. The company of wealthy people opens a person up to coveting what they have. When it comes to the Hereafter, it is better to associate with people who are superior to you in their desire for and understanding of it.

Companionship yields two kinds of impact: one that drags a person down to the compost of the world and the other that points toward God, the Exalted, and an existence that lasts forever. A companion who tries to sell the ephemeral stuff of this life and makes it the substance of conversation and pursuit is dragging the soul earthward. It is better, beyond compare, to seek out the company of those who help one achieve contentment with God. When one is content, little will suffice. But without contentment, nothing suffices.

Imam Mawlūd says that seeking refuge with God is the most efficacious treatment for all diseases of the heart. Sīdī Ibn ᶜĀshir says, "The only real cure for all these diseases is to go to God with complete unconditional imploring." What is meant here is urgently seeking refuge in God's protection and guidance, to seek this as if one were holding onto a thread over a canyon. It is begging, which before God is honorable. Most converts to Islam have said that before they became Muslims, they reached a point in their lives in which they petitioned with all their heart and emotion that God guide them. In the haze of confusion and spiritual morass, they literally begged for it: "Just show me what to do!" Afterwards, it became easy and the path very clear. This is what Imam Mawlūd is suggesting. There is nothing nonchalant in this act.

Imam Mawlūd says that one should be like a person drowning in the sea or stranded in a desert without any provision. A moment of desperation can often be the best thing that ever happens to a person. Yusuf Islam (formerly Cat Stevens), the philanthropist, musician, and educator, says that he once was drowning in the Pacific Ocean near Malibu, California. In desperation, he called out to God to save him, and said that if He would do so, he would seek out His guidance. The very waves and undercurrents of the ocean that nearly killed him were transformed into a force that propelled him back to shore. True to his word and promise, Yusuf indeed sought God's religion and embraced Islam.

Also Ibn Abī Jahl was on a boat with Abyssinian Christians. He fell into the water and was about to drown when he called upon the idol Hubal. The Christians on the boat said, "Are you calling on an idol in Mecca to help you?" Right then he realized how foolish it was. The truth about the oneness of God entered his heart.

Beneficial Actions for Purifying the Heart

POEM VERSES 176–179

As for action that is beneficial in purifying the heart, none is more effective than what is consistent, even if it is slight.

Include also action that is done in the absence of witnesses, or action done purely for His love or out of awe of His majesty.

The purest deed is that done by someone free of worldly wants. The opposite of this is the deed of the covetous one whose endeavors are ultimately insignificant.

The actions of those who strive out of hope are more resplendent and exalted than one whose striving is compelled by fear.

Discussion

When speaking of the purification of the heart, it is important to know that "purification" is not a state, but an ongoing process. Just as we go through a day careful about our bodily cleanliness, we must similarly tend to our spiritual purity, for purification and sincerity do not survive a passive relationship. They are not qualities that are ignited and glow on without attendance. For this reason Imam Mawlūd states that what is most beneficial for the purification of the heart are those acts that are done with consistency, even if they are small. This is based on the statement of the Prophet ﷺ: "The best actions are the continuous ones, even if they are slight." It's like silverware: one may polish it with a few hard strokes and then put it down; or one may gently polish it regularly so that its shimmer is maintained. Left unattended, the heart becomes encrusted. Unwholesome deeds accumulate and take away its purity. But with consistent work on self-purification, the heart becomes cleansed and is kept that way.

The Companions of the Prophet ﷺ were consistent with their actions once they commenced them. Once a Companion asked the Prophet ﷺ to recommend a fast. The Prophet ﷺ said, "Fast three days out of the month," which are the middle days of the month when the moon is the fullest. This first recommendation of the Prophet ﷺ was moderate, for the way of the Prophet ﷺ was moderation. However, the Companion responded, "I can do more." Hence, the Prophet ﷺ advised, "Then fast Mondays and Thursdays." However, the Companion indicated that he is able to fast even more. The Prophet ﷺ then said, "Then fast every other day," which is the Fast of David ﷷ, "and do not exceed this." Hence, the Companion started to fast every other day and kept it throughout his life. When he reached old age, however, he realized that he should have accepted the Prophet's first recommendation and have fasted only three days a month, as the fasting had now become difficult for him. Scholars have commented that when the Prophet's Companions took on supererogatory rites of worship (*nawāfil*), they did so for the duration of their lives. It was something they embraced as a spiritual practice, and they did not abandon it. This is not to say that this is an obligation. However, if people wish to climb straight and right in their spiritual journey, their acts of worship should be regular and consistent.

The Prophet ﷺ was a universal prophet, which means, among other things, that he was an example for all people. He fasted and broke his fasts. He prayed and rested. The life of Prophet ﷺ has something for people of diverse strengths and weaknesses—for everyone. For example, God opens the hearts of some people so that they incline to perform night prayer. For others, He opens their hearts to recitation of the Qur'an. For others yet, it may be that they are inclined towards being generous. Others may find their hearts inclining towards consistent remembrance of God. Fasting is the love and passion of some people. And others love memorizing hadith and teaching it. There is much in Islam and in the beautiful model of the Prophet ﷺ that one may learn from. Very rarely do we find a person who encompasses all (or even most) of his qualities. However, if a person finds himself inclining to a certain supererogatory worship rite, he should follow it and remain consistent in its practice. Imam Mālik said,

God has opened up for His servants doors of goodness: for some He opens doors of fasting; for others He opens doors of charity; others yet, doors of knowledge and teaching; and for others, doors of abstinence and contentment. And I am pleased with what God has opened up for me in educating people.

Imam Mawlūd says that one should consciously perform devotional deeds in the absence of witnesses. If one gives charity openly, this is good, but in secret it is better. This protects against ostentation. Fuḍayl ibn ʿIyāḍ was once walking down a street and someone said, "There goes a man who spends the whole night in prayer." Fuḍayl began to weep: "I cannot remember spending one full night in prayer. How greatly God has honored me in making people think I am better than what I know myself to be."

An act of worship done for the love of God is a higher station than those acts done out of fear of Hellfire. This is a common understanding among scholars throughout the ages, including Imam al-Ghazālī. This view does not belittle the fear of punishment, but it does assign a higher station to guiding one's conduct out of awe of God and a heightened sense of His majesty and greatness.

The ascetic (*zāhid*) acts for no other reason than the pleasure and love of God. This is the highest action. Asceticism in Islam differs from other traditions. In Islam, the essence of asceticism is a lack of want. The ascetic is the one who does not have attachment in his heart for material things. Many Companions of the Prophet ﷺ were wealthy, but, like ʿAbd al-Raḥmān ibn ʿAwf, they were also considered *zāhid* despite their wealth.

Imam Mawlūd says that striving with the energy of hope is more exalted than being compelled by fear. This is especially true when the benefits of one's acts touch the lives of others, which is the case with charity (*ṣadaqah*) for the needy. There is so much hope in Islam; its creed and ethos are rife with optimism and buoyancy. Planting a tree from which birds eat reaps the planter reward so long as that tree stands. Hope is light: "*Indeed, in the Messenger of God there is an excellent model for you—for whoever is hopeful of God and the Last Day and remembers God much*" (QUR'AN, 33:21).

POEM VERSES 180–188

Of particular benefit is that which extends beyond the individual or is difficult for the self—such as a glutton's fast,

Or the years of youth spent in avoiding wrongs and in willing obedience, or the contributions of a miser from the best of his wealth when he is of sound mind, seeking thereby the pleasure of God with absolute sincerity.

All of these purify the heart. Moreover, doing a good deed which one conceals is also purifying; and the best of endeavors is one that purifies the heart.

Likewise, the most harmful of wrongs is what hardens the heart and was done with consistency or [the doer] taking joy in doing it. Sages have preferred a wrong that engenders humility to a right that clothes one in a gown of self-righteous arrogance.

An atom's weight of exalted praiseworthy action from the heart—like contentment with what one has, detachment from worldly things, and reliance [upon God]—

Is better in God's sight than high mountains of external actions [without sincerity].

Indeed, leaving a dollar because it is from a prohibited source is better than giving much in charity and [better than] several pilgrimages.

Discussion

The Imam advises also to seek out acts that are trying to the soul. The example he gives is fasting for the glutton, one who has a difficult time controlling his or her food intake. The principle applies to the miser who is blessed enough to recognize his shortcoming, that he should battle his soul by giving charity, detaching himself from his want of wealth and its hoarding, no matter the internal resistance. The Prophet ﷺ said that the best charity is charity given when one is in good health and sound condition and fears poverty. Thus, the miser should give to cleanse his heart of miserliness; and the fear of poverty should not prevent him from giving.

Imam Mawlūd mentions this in combination with youth who spend their formative years in the shade of guidance. There are, of course, people who spent much of their lives doing things they should not have but then turn around when they grow old. Some will say that, in general, their station is not equal to those who were morally circumspect and diligent in their worship throughout their lives. Repentance is easier for older people who have lost something of their vigor. This is not to say that their penitence is not real.

An abominable attitude somehow survives in some parts of the Muslim world. It basically states that the year of responsibility is age forty, and that before that age, one may do as he wills. This is based on the fact that the Prophet ﷺ received revelation at that age. However, this idea is entirely ignorant and vacuous. It is also morally and spiritually devastating. Who can guarantee lengthy life? And who can guarantee one will actually turn to repentance after years of disobedience? To intentionally wreak moral havoc in anticipation of repenting late is untenable.

The Imam says next that the worst things a person can do are those acts that harden the heart. One of them is speaking a lot without mentioning God. Jesus ؑ warned, "Do not sit in a gathering without mentioning God, for a gathering in which God is not mentioned will harden the heart." The more the tongue is occupied in remembering God, the softer the heart becomes—imbued with compassion, mercy, and love.

Imam Mawlūd says next, “An atom’s weight of high praiseworthy action from the heart is better than high mountains of external actions with no heart.” He then paraphrases what Imam Saḥnūn said, “Leaving one penny from what God has made forbidden is better than going to pilgrimage 70,000 times.”

The Root of All Diseases of the Heart

POEM VERSES 189–196

The root cause of all of these diseases is love of the temporal world. This is the opinion of both al-Hilālī and Ibn ʿĀshir.

Ibn ʿAṭā'allāh, on the other hand, considered the root cause of every disease to be man's self-satisfaction.

Likewise, the root cause of all good qualities is the lack of self-satisfaction. And this conclusion is obvious

Because being [dissatisfied with oneself] prompts you to seek virtuous character and to vigilantly avoid what is inappropriate.

The origin of either of these states relates to the company one keeps [from either camp], for a man's character is that of the company he keeps.

Thus, if a man achieves any state, inevitably his companions will be affected by it.

For this reason, Luqmān, the full moon of wisdom, advised his son to keep close company with the people of knowledge.

He compared the effect of the reviving light of wisdom upon the heart to that of a lush downpour upon the barren earth.

Discussion

The comprehensive root of the heart's diseases, according to Imam Mawlūd, is love of the temporal world, which he cites as the opinion of Imam al-Hilālī and Imam Ibn ʿĀshir. Ibn ʿAbbās said that it was covetousness (*ṭamaʿ*). There are differences of opinion regarding the mother cause of diseases of the heart, but their differences are shades of understanding rather than alternate paradigms. When Imam Ibn ʿĀshir says that it is the love of power and authority, it comes down to love of the world. What is power and authority other than branches of the world?

Imam Ibn ʿAṭā'allāh, who is often quoted in this book and mentioned by name in this passage of Imam Mawlūd's poem, was a master of the science of the heart. His book of aphorisms is one of the most highly regarded masterpieces in Islamic spiritual tradition. His 35th aphorism in that collection reads,

The source of every disobedience, indifference, and passion is self-satisfaction. The source of every obedience, vigilance, and virtue is dissatisfaction with one's self. It is better for you to keep company with an ignorant man dissatisfied with himself than to keep company with a learned man satisfied with himself. For what knowledge is there in a self-satisfied scholar? And what ignorance is there in an unlearned man dissatisfied with himself?

Nowadays, there is an urgency to root out the feeling of shame. There are self-help books to show how to excise this out of the soul. However, dissatisfaction with oneself is the very thing that causes people to reflect and reevaluate, which is requisite for spiritual success. Shame and dissatisfaction can be moral lifesavers. (Shame is different from low self-esteem, in which one feels contempt for himself.)

Sīdī Aḥmad Zarrūq said that there are three signs of being overly content with the soul. First is being sensitive to one's own rights and indifferent to the rights of others. In Islam, one's responsibilities preponderate over one's rights. The second sign is ignoring one's own faults, as if one has none, while being preoccupied with the faults of others. A poet once said, "A contented eye does not see faults." The third sign is giving oneself too much leniency.

Sīdī Aḥmad Zarrūq then said that there are three signs that someone is not content with himself. First is when a person checks himself, is self-accusing, and wary of his intentions. Joseph ﷺ, who was known for his exceptional purity, said, "*I do not declare myself innocent, but the soul often commands evil, except upon one whom my Lord has mercy*" (QUR'AN, 12:53). One should ask oneself, "Am I doing this for show or for the sake of God?"

Second is being careful of the blemishes of the soul. The Prophet ﷺ supplicated, "O God, do not leave me to the soul even for a blink of an eye."

Third is forcing the self to do difficult things, such as eating less and spending money in charity. Abū ʿUthmān said, "Whoever sees anything good about himself has not seen the faults of his soul." ʿĀ'ishah ﷺ was honored in being the wife of the Prophet ﷺ. She was beautiful and one of the most brilliant women in history. She was from an excellent family. With all these assets, she said, "I deem myself so insignificant that I would never think Qur'an would be revealed about me." (This is in regard to the episode in which the hypocrites accused her of a sin. God, the Exalted, revealed her innocence in the Qur'an.) She was humble, but she wasn't a woman with low self-esteem. She obviously had striking self-confidence. She was regularly asked questions because of her knowledge of the Qur'an.

Being vigilant about one's own faults does not amount to self-loathing or depletion of confidence. In fact, confidence gives one the courage to find fault in oneself.

A poet once said, "I never saw a fault from among the faults of humanity like the sloth of people capable of human perfection." One reason talented people become underachievers is that they are too satisfied with themselves. A master of any craft is not one who achieves a certain level of proficiency and stops, but one who is committed to constant improvement.

Imam Mawlūd says that dissatisfaction is a motivator to seek out better character. A human being is spiritually stalled as long as he is content and smug with his state. The basis of achieving good is knowing oneself. When this happens, a person becomes aware of his imperfections, minor and major, and is ashamed of them to the point he strives to replace them with generosity, agreeableness, honesty, reliability, dignity, and other noble traits.

When the mind is given the responsibility to decide upon right and wrong, it usually bases its judgment subjectively: what advances or thwarts one's whims? Our understanding of right and wrong, licit and illicit, needs a judge higher than ourselves and our whims. We are beings who have been created and, therefore, have a Creator who brought us into existence for a reason. It is His purpose and guidance that informs our sensitivity and response to right and wrong.

Imam Mawlūd states that diseases and blessings are related to the company one keeps. The Prophet ﷺ said, "A man takes on the religion of his companion." The company of a person who delays or neglects prayer, or a person who abandons paying zakat, or a person who is promiscuous drags others into his way of life. Conversely, the company of a righteous person will pull one upward. As it is said, "If you sit at the door of a tavern, you will either walk in and partake or merely smell the stench of alcohol and drunkards. But if you sit at the door of a perfumer, you will either walk in and wear the scent or at least enjoy the fragrance."

The learned are like rain that quickens a lifeless land. Sitting with esteemed company enlivens the heart and makes it more fertile for the growth of faith (*imān*). It will take one from six detrimental things to six beneficial things: doubt to certainty; ostentation in acts to sincerity; heedlessness to remembrance; desire for this world to desire for the Hereafter; arrogance to humbleness; and a bad internal nature to an excellent one. Imam Ibn ʿAṭā'allāh advised the same: "Do not take as a companion someone whose state will not elevate you and whose speech does not direct you to God."

POEM VERSES 197–204

Remember God much, and know that the Qur'an is the best of it. This rule excludes those times when other types [of remembrance] have been prescribed.

Begin by asking for forgiveness and benedictions upon [Prophet Muḥammad ﷺ], our guide to all good things.

Have the same reverence [during remembrance] as you would during prayer and guard yourself from any mispronunciations, for that is among the prohibitions.

Whoever adds a long vowel, for instance, after the ha' *in* ilāha *when he is saying* lā ilāha illā l-lāh, *or adds a vowel to the hamzah at the onset of the word*

Has committed a wrong deed, according to the consensus of the righteous people. Furthermore, he has worshipped God but did so disobediently [by his neglect of tajwīd*].*[1]

This is what has been clearly stated in [the book] al-Khazīnah *by one whose speech has been illuminated by serenity.*

It is necessary when engaged in remembrance that every letter be pronounced with precision in terms of its origin and linguistic attributes.

The most virtuous form of devotion is contemplative reflection and the best of that is annihilation of the self, which is the supreme station.

Discussion

Imam Mawlūd speaks next of the importance of *dhikr*, the remembrance of God, which is vital to the cure of each disease of the heart (and society). He mentions the exceptional excellence of reciting the Qur'an. For example, reciting Sura al-Ikhlaṣ (the 112th sura of the Qur'an), along with the closing suras of the Qur'an (together known as *al-muʿawwadhatān*, the "two suras of refuge"), three times each, is highly recommended. When one recites while reflecting deeply on the meaning of the words, doors of insight open and one's faith (*imān*) grows stronger.

---

1 Qur'anic recitation and prayers can only be done according to the rules of orthophonics (*tajwīd*). To do so, neglecting the rules, is sinful. Imam al-Jazarī says in his famous didactic poem, "The rules of *tajwīd* are necessary – whoever recites without them is sinful."

It is better to recite from the copy of the Qur'an itself than from memorization, since it involves the eyes, hands, and ears. (When driving a car, recitation by memorization is obviously the choice.) It is said that Imam Aḥmad ibn Hanbal had 99 dreams about God, the Exalted. In one of them, he asked the Almighty about all the things that draw a worshipper near to Him: Which of them was the greatest? He was told it was the recitation of Qur'an. "With or without comprehension?" he asked. The reply was, "With or without comprehension." Not understanding the language of the Qur'an should not bar one from receiving the blessings in this exalted practice. The authority of this position is not borrowed from the dream of a great man, but it is corroborated by proofs offered by many scholars throughout the ages. The only time when the Qur'an is not the preferred *dhikr* is when other obligations are immediately pressing.

Imam Mawlūd states that the remembrance of God is essential in taking the spiritual path. The Messenger of God ﷺ said, "The likeness of the one who remembers his Lord and one who does not remember his Lord is like the living and the dead." Someone who remembers God has a heart that is alive and busy with the best of deeds. A hadith states, "Make remembrance of God until they say, 'He is a mad man.'" If people come across a Muslim who moves his lips in God's remembrance, the first thing that may come to their minds is that he is not altogether sane. The Prophet ﷺ said to his Companions, "Shall I not inform you of the best of your deeds and the purest of them in the sight of your Lord and the most exalted of them in rank, and what is better for you than spending gold and silver and better for you than encountering your enemy in battle, where you strike them and they strike you?" His Companions answered, "Yes, of course!" He told them, "It is the remembrance of God." Scholars have explained how the remembrance of God exceeds in merit even jihad explaining that *dhikr* is an end, while jihad is a means to removing aggression. It is generally known that the ends are higher than the means, for we were created to remember God, and all else that we do is in order to establish the conditions that permit this remembrance.

God has said, "*Remember Me; I will remember you*" (QUR'AN, 2:152). There is also a hadith that states that whoever remembers his Lord, God remembers him, and whomever God remembers, he is enriched in this world and in the Hereafter and is in need of nothing. One of the great things about *dhikr* is that it is different from other acts of worship, like Pilgrimage and prayer. Remembrance is not time restricted; it is associated with all aspects of life, such as meals, getting dressed, traveling, retiring for sleep, even sexual intimacy (for which there is a known supplication), and the like. It is said that when one is in the state of remembrance, any affliction that comes to him or her raises that person's rank, and if one dies in the state of remembrance, he or she dies as a martyr. Also, if one's last words are, "There is no deity but God," he or she enters Heaven.

Imam Mawlūd says that in making remembrance, one should start with seeking God's forgiveness (*istighfār*) for his or her neglect and misdeeds, past or immediate. *Istighfār* is the process of asking God to remit our sins and cleanse us of their ill effects. One should say, for example, at least 100 times in a day "*astaghfiru l-lāh*," which means, "I seek forgiveness from God." One should also begin with benedictions on the Prophet ﷺ, that is, asking God to bless him and grant him peace. Many scholars have specified benediction of the Prophet ﷺ as particularly effective because it is a prayer that is guaranteed to be answered by God. In fact, the Qur'an states, "*Indeed, God and His angels bless the Prophet. O you who believe, bless him and salute him with a worthy salutation*" (QUR'AN. 33:56). What is meant by the angels blessing the Prophet ﷺ is their constant supplication to God to send His peace and blessings upon His beloved Messenger ﷺ. Moreover, the command to believers also references their supplication to God that He send blessings to the Prophet ﷺ.

Whoever prays for the Prophet ﷺ one time, God prays on that person ten times. The Prophet ﷺ said, "Prayer on the Messenger of God is light in this world, light in the grave, and light on the Traverse [in the Hereafter]." The Prophet ﷺ was aware of his station as the Seal of the Prophets, and he believed in what God has revealed to him, as the Qur'an states (QUR'AN, 2:285). He was unabashed in relating to his Companions (and all the generations after them) what will be of benefit to them in this life and the next, including invoking prayers of blessing upon him. Such prayers, as he has said, shall be a light when we need light the most, in the dark grave and on the Traverse, the bridge that crosses over Hellfire, over which everyone must cross. It is also light in the heart.

When praying on the Prophet ﷺ, one should have the same reverence and comportment that one has when performing other *dhikr*, like having ablution (*wuḍū'*) and facing toward the direction of Mecca (the qiblah) when possible. What is recommended for prayer (*ṣalāh*) is recommended for *dhikr*: cleanliness, perfume, and cleaning the teeth with a tooth-stick (*siwāk*). When one says "*lā ilāha illā l-lāh*" (there is no deity but God), he negates polytheism and idolatry. If one says "*al-ḥamdu li l-lāh*" (all praise is for God), he is reminded of the constant blessings that God has bestowed. When one says "*lā ḥawla wa lā qūwata illā billāh*" (there is no might or power except with God), he disengages himself of any illusion of having power, for all of it is with God. When one prays on the Prophet ﷺ, it is appropriate to imagine the Prophet ﷺ teaching us guidance and the proper way to worship—essential teachings that we never would have learned had he not taught us. We must also remember God's love for him.

Imam Mawlūd states that when engaged in remembrance it is important to pronounce the words well and to avoid incorrect pronunciation to the best of one's ability. Mispronunciation of some words can change their meaning. Sīdī ʿAbd Allāh Ould Ḥajj Ibrāhīm said in his book *Khazīnah al-Asrār* (*Storehouse of Secrets*) that when one engages in remembrance he should do so with every letter. One should not drag his tongue lazily, especially in reciting the Qur'an. Proper pronunciation lends itself to deeper comprehension of what one is saying. For those who have difficulty in pronouncing some of the letters, they, of course, can still engage in remembrance, doing their best with matters of pronunciation.

To reflect on God's creation is known as a great act of worship, a practice that helps a person see the signs—those glimpses of the unseen purposely placed in the physical world so that we may be increased in faith and certitude. This meditative contemplation, as Imam Mawlūd states, is the most virtuous of devotions. Those inclined to reflection are known as people of understanding and are described as those who remember God while *standing, sitting, or lying on their sides*. As they reflect on the creation of the heavens and the earth, they say, "*Our Lord, You have not created this in vain. Glory be to You!*" (QUR'AN, 3:191). This combines remembrance of God with a presence of heart and mind that augments the power of remembrance. There is a hadith that states, "To reflect for one hour is better than a year in worship."

The objects of reflection (*tafakkur*) are many. One may reflect on the verses of the Qur'an. Another may reflect on the signs of God in creation or reflect on the promise of God, the reward that He guarantees believers who are patient and obedient. Such reflection creates ardent desire and hope for Paradise with its unfathomable bliss, peace, provision, landscapes, and excellent company. Likewise, one reflects on the punishment God has promised those who choose wickedness over purity, misguidance over guidance, and corruption over wholesomeness. Reflecting on the terrors of the grave and the horrors of Hell instills the kind of dread that strengthens a person's resolve to never stray from the path of God. When we reflect on all that God has given us that infinitely exceeds the measure of what we deserve, and then reflect on what little is required from us, this extinguishes self-righteousness and arrogance and increases gratitude.

People ask about those who engage in a great deal of remembrance yet neglect or ignore the obligatory rites of worship as if they have transcended the need for these rites. This is unmitigated ignorance. The first and foremost obligation on every human being is to gain knowledge. A human being is nothing until he has learned what is obligatory on every individual (*farḍ ʿayn*). Without this, a person has no rank or standing with regard to God, and nothing is more consequential to a person other than his or her standing with God. When God created us, He gave us accountability and the means and ability to carry out our responsibilities. Anyone who does not care to learn the first order of knowledge is living the life of a farm animal, a creature that does nothing but graze in this life, which is entirely insufficient in God's sight.

Shaykh Ould al-Khadīm has mentioned the names of many renowned scholars of the past who were learned in the outward and inner sciences, the latter being Sufism (*taṣawwuf*). These scholars say that before *taṣawwuf*, there must be sacred law. *Taṣawwuf* without law will lead one astray.

There is a confused sense of spirituality in which one feels he or she can attain to level of perceiving reality fully without tending to the responsibilities and obligations of the shariah. This is a misleading phenomenon that spreads because of its appeal: spiritual sensation without any moral obligation. A person on this path may do as he or she wills and take solace in pseudo-sensations. This virulent trend seizes people and whisks them away from the truth, although they feel quite content. Islam does not call people to unreasoned faith. It demands that a person learn authentic knowledge, which buttresses true spiritual growth. This real spirituality is protected by the shariah, just as a shell protects its fruit. If one removes the husk, the ear is exposed and it begins to rot. A person who tries to attain spirituality without the shariah will eventually destroy his soul and become, in essence, a false person. There are people who outwardly don the mantle and comportment of spiritual enlightenment, but who are filled with diseases of the heart.

We must remember that if a person has done wrong, the spiritual path is not severed. There is the recourse of seeking repentance from God. One should not confess or broadcast what he or she has done. If God has veiled one's wrongdoing, do not tear the veil down. There is a hadith in which a man came to the Prophet ﷺ and said, "I committed a sin," and he meant adultery. "So punish me." But the Prophet ﷺ turned and walked away. The man pursued the Prophet ﷺ and told him again that he wanted to be punished for his sin. The Prophet ﷺ finally looked at him and asked him if he made ablution and prayed. He was telling him that Islam purifies. The Prophet ﷺ said, "Whoever does indecency, let him veil his acts with the veiling of God and let him make repentance." He also said, "Whoever comes to our faces and admits them, then we will punish them."

Therefore, there is no better treatment for the diseases of the heart than remembrance. Most of the other recommended cures either touch upon or include the remembrance of God as essential. It has been said, "When we are ill, we treat ourselves with Your remembrance. And when we abandon Your remembrance, we relapse into illness."

The consultative body of ʿUmar ibn al-Khaṭṭāb included a man whose cousin insisted on meeting with ʿUmar. When he was given the opportunity, he demanded from ʿUmar, "Give me something from what God gave you [meaning money] because you're someone who hasn't given out much, and you do not judge with justice." When ʿUmar heard this, he grew angry. But the man's cousin intervened and cited a verse to ʿUmar, "*Turn away from the ignorant*" (QUR'AN, 7:199). ʿUmar's anger immediately subsided, even though the man had insulted him, lied, and disrespected Islamic authority. Citing the verse was the remembrance of God, which calmed ʿUmar down.

Many passages of the Qur'an encourage or command humanity to remember God as often as possible. The Qur'an says that in the Messenger of God ﷺ we have an excellent model (QUR'AN, 33:21). The people who benefit most from this model are those who engage in remembrance frequently, which was the way of the Prophet ﷺ. The Arabic word *tazkiyyah* means to purify oneself, but it also means to grow. God, the Exalted, says that had it not been for His favor upon us, not one of us would have become purified or would have enjoyed growth (QUR'AN, 24:21). Thus, purification comes about as the result of the spiritual work that God, the Exalted, has graciously blessed humanity with, and *dhikr* plays a major role in that.

ʿUmar once wrote to his governors: "I consider prayer to be the most important deed in your life. So whoever guards and is vigilant in his prayer, he has guarded his religion. And whoever is negligent about his prayer, he will neglect matters of lesser importance." What is great about this counsel is that it offers clarity about priorities. Remembrance (*dhikr*) is a practice that is validated only by the performance of the obligatory rites of worship, including ritual prayer (*ṣalāh*). If a person stays up all night thumbing his beads but sleeps past dawn prayer, he has done no service to himself. Hence, the foremost thing a person needs to guard is the prayer and its requirements, like ablution (*wuḍū'*).

A Muslim tradition reports that Prophet David ﷺ saw a group of men remembering God and was impressed with them, but it was revealed to him that these men were of no worth in the sight of God because if a woman had come along and offered herself to any of them, they would have accepted her offer.

The best of worship occurs with the combination of speech and reflection. When practiced for a long time regularly, one achieves what is called *fanā'* in Sufi terminology. Imam al-Junayd is said to have coined the term, which literally means extinction. When it comes to the world of remembrance, it includes achieving supreme realizations about God, the Exalted, and His acts. When one reflects deeply, he separates himself from others and even from his own limitations.

Imam al-Junayd says that in deep spiritual practice there can be profound experiences. An example of one is a *ḥāl*, which is an overwhelming spiritual state that is uncontrollable. The scholars of this science differentiate between *ḥāl* and *maqām*. *Maqām* is more or less a fixed condition or station, whereas a *ḥāl* is a temporary state, a momentary burst of spiritual epiphany. For example, the station of repentance (*maqām al-tawbah*) is one in which one cannot willingly be disobedient to God. But the *ḥāl* of repentance is when someone becomes so overwhelmed with remorse over what he had done wrong in the past, he rushes to God, the Exalted, and profoundly seeks His forgiveness with a powerful sense of God's presence. It is an inrush that comes into the heart, filling it with light and spiritual expansion. It is highest when one is not aware of himself, only of God and His attributes. This kind of extinction of the soul is caused by one's focus and heightened spiritual experience.

Our objective is not merely to go through these spiritual experiences, but to be firmly grounded in a path that takes us to the pleasure of God and salvation in the Hereafter. If one performs remembrance properly and often, things will happen to the inner self. These things are studied by scholars of the inner sciences. But we're also aware that Satan can play games with those who engage in certain practices blindly and without knowledge and prioritization. That's the peril of New Age practices and philosophies that can lead to sensations and experiences in which the one having them cannot distinguish between satanic influences, psychological phenomena, and true spiritual encounters.

Fanā' alludes to something altogether different. It is founded on the sources of Islam and the tutelage of learned people who have knowledge of both the shariah and spiritual matters. The person who is doing *dhikr* with reflection loses awareness of himself. There are authentic reports of the Companions of the Prophet ﷺ and other righteous people of later generations who, as they stood in prayer, were completely unaware of their surroundings. If a person is sincere in remembering God, then God may bless him or her with an "opening," that is, a deeper witnessing of God Himself.

There is a hadith in which God says,

> My servant does not draw near to Me by anything more beloved to Me than what is obligatory upon him, and he will continue to draw near to Me with the supererogatory acts of worship until I love him. And when I love him I become the eye with which he sees, the ear with which he hears, the tongue with which he speaks, and the hand with which he grasps, and if he seeks refuge in Me I give him refuge with Me, and if he asks of Me, I give him.

This hadith does not mean that God, the Exalted, takes on human qualities. Muslims do not believe in divine incarnation or God becoming creation. However, we do believe that the human being can be in a profound state of awareness of God's action in creation. The whole world is an act of God and people can go into a state of absolute witnessing where they see everything as being acts of God. They do not see otherness and thus they recognize the Reality behind it. For this reason, the believer sees good in all things, even in affliction and trial, in which there is wisdom: an opportunity to grow, purify oneself, learn patience, and draw near to God. "*It may be that you dislike something, though it is good for you. And it may be that you love something, though it is bad for you*" (QUR'AN, 2:216). Understanding this is the idea in witnessing God's wisdom in events of the world.

Qadi Abū Bakr Ibn al-ʿArabī said that Satan's foremost objective with the believer is to separate him from the remembrance of God, the Exalted. But if Satan finds believers doing much remembrance, then he will try to turn them away from the remembrance of God that is taken from the Qur'an and the supplications and formulas stated by the Prophet ﷺ himself. Sīdī Aḥmad Zarrūq said that one should say the litanies that the Prophet ﷺ used to say, especially those that he said often. One should do this before those supplications composed from other people. It is permissible to read supplication of others as long as they are knowledgeable and known for their piety. Even here, preference (after the words of the Qur'an and the Prophet ﷺ) should be given to the words of the Companions and the Successors (*tābiʿūn*).

Here we end the translation and commentary of the portion of Imam Mawlūd's poem that deals with various diseases of the heart. The appendices that follow delve into issues previously mentioned but with greater detail and further explanation.

Appendix One

Remembrance

Taken from the *Wird* of Imām ʿAbdallāh al-Ḥaddād

Imam ʿAbdallāh al-Ḥaddād was a Yemeni scholar and a man of great spiritual insight. I am grateful that his descendant was my teacher. I learned from him that it is excellent to begin one's *dhikr* with the *basmala* (*Bismillahi-rahmani-rahim* or "In the name of God, the Merciful, the Mercy-Giving"). The Prophet ﷺ said that any act that does not begin in the name of God is severed from goodness. The Imam then would recite Sūrat al-Ikhlāṣ three times. The Prophet ﷺ said that this sūrah is equivalent to reciting one-third of the Qur'an. The sūrah should be read preferably after every prayer and in the morning and evening. Next, the concluding two sūrahs of the Qur'an should be read, Sūrat al-Falaq (113) and Sūrat al-Nās (114), which give protection, by God's leave. They should also be recited everyday. There is a hadith that says they should be recited before going to sleep.

The Prophet ﷺ often prayed for protection from Satan and his evil promptings: "O God, I seek refuge in You from Satan the accursed, from his promptings, inspirations." Also, *Say, "My Lord, I seek refuge in You from the urgings of the devils"* (QUR'AN, 23:97). *Urgings* here is *hamazāt*, which means to goad someone to do something that he or she shouldn't do. One of the signs of the end of time is that the minds of people will become full of whisperings. People today are constantly fed messages that ask them to do something, whether to buy a product or revel in the beat of a song or agree to its message. Music, television, internet, cellular phones (with internet access), and films are so ubiquitous, one has to forcibly alienate himself from popular culture to find solace.

Evil whisperings and suggestions can come in a variety of forms, visual and audible. They go to the heart, especially when people are not circumspect as to what they permit into their souls. Over time suggestions build up to the point one can no longer discern what is real or a fraud, what is beneficial or ruinous. Hearts are destroyed this way. Seemingly innocent facets of our lives can exhaust a person's time with trivial matters. The whole culture of sports enthusiasm can lead to an incredible loss of time passively watching the competition. When one wastes time, the heart becomes complacent and lazy.

Once we realize that we are accountable for our entire life, then every minute becomes vital. Time is the gift God has given us. And what we do with it is the most important challenge that faces us. This is not to suggest that recreation is at odds with *īmān*. People who fail to take some form of recreation will impair both their physical and mental health. But the warning here is about something different: it is about the way things are today, in which millions of people *live* to be entertained, as if this is the purpose of their lives. It addresses the cultural war cry, "Work for the weekend," as if the purpose of the weekdays is merely to bankroll the entertainment of the weekends. People who are serious about spiritual health (about being a successful human being) need to wean themselves from the *culture of fun*.

Do you think that We created you in vain and that you will never return to Us? Exalted is God, the King, the Truth. There is no God but Him, Lord of the Noble Throne (QUR'AN, 23:115-16). The Prophet ﷺ often recited these verses. He would also recite, *Lord, forgive and have mercy, You are the best of those who show mercy* (QUR'AN, 23:118); *Glory be to God in your evenings and in your mornings. All praise is His in the heavens and the earth and at the setting of the sun and at noonday* (QUR'AN, 30:17-18).

God says, *Had We sent down this Qur'an upon a mountain, you would have seen it humbled, rent asunder by the fear of God* (QUR'AN, 59:21). The word *khashyah* is *fear* that emanates from knowledge, not of the unknown. The implication of the Qur'an being revealed is in itself awesome enough to reduce a mountain to dust. It is the last of God's revelations, the final heavenly message, thus fulfilling God's covenant to guide humanity. The content of the Book reveals so much about God, the reality of existence, the purpose of life, and the Hereafter, no one can ever claim ignorance.

Obviously, *dhikr* should include reflective recitation of the Qur'an, a practice that leads to awe, fear, reverence, and humility—lights of character for the human soul. God the Exalted says, *And We set forth these examples for people so that they may reflect* (QUR'AN, 59:21). God offered the trust of faith and accountability to the heavens, the earth, and the mountains, but they refused because of the enormity of the responsibility.

The most excellent names of God *(asmā'allāh al-ḥusnā)* are a wellspring of spiritual enlightenment. Scholars have encouraged reflection on the names of God as a priceless form of *dhikr*. The traditional count of God's names is ninety-nine, all of which are in the Qur'an.

He is God, there is no God but Him, Knower of the unseen and the seen. He is the Merciful, the Mercy-Giving. He is God, besides whom there is no God, the King, the Holy, the Complete, the Source of Security, the Guardian, the Overpowering, the August, the Proud. Transcendent is God over what they associate [with Him]. He is God, the Creator, the Maker, the Fashioner. His are the most excellent names. All that is in the heavens and the earth glorifies Him. And He is the Overpowering, the All-Wise (QUR'AN, 59:22-24).

This passage is celebrated for the names it reveals of God. He is the *Knower of the unseen and the seen*. The Arabic word for *seen* here is *shahādah*, which literally means *testimony*, for every *seen* thing testifies to God's oneness. A poet once said, "How wondrous that man can deny God, while in every movement and stillness there is a witness and everything in creation testifies that God is one." When one says, *Subḥān Allāh (Transcendent is God)*, it is an affirmation that there is nothing comparable to God, who is completely free of any imperfection and is wholly transcendent, exalted beyond what mortals attribute to Him and beyond what even the learned know of Him. God determines that He will bring a human being into existence. This is God as *al-Khāliq (Creator)*. It is His profound wisdom that the union of the male and female gametes in the womb of the woman be the way in which this creation takes place. This is God as *al-Bārī' (Maker)*. Those cells that result from this union differentiate and form the various parts of the body. The central nervous system becomes distinguished from the respiratory organs. Mounds of somites on the flanks of the fetus differentiate and form the hundreds of separate muscles in the body, as nerves and blood vessels follow them. The clumps at the end of the arms endure a specific and detailed pattern of cell death, and behold fingers appear. Further, each fingerprint, each DNA, each human face is different from others. This is God as *al-Muṣawwir (Fashioner)*.

All the separate names of God do not suggest that there is a linearity to God the Exalted. It is for human benefit that God's attributes are set in identifiable words that we may understand. Imam al-Ghazālī says that because human beings can only look at things from one aspect at a time, we require such revelations from the unseen. God is one in essence and attribute, and eternally so.

We live in the age of Noah ﷺ in the sense that a flood of distraction accosts us. It is a slow and subtle drowning. For those who notice it, they engage in the remembrance of God. The rites of worship and devotion to God's remembrance *(dhikr)* are planks of the ark. When Noah ﷺ started to build his ark, his people mocked him and considered him a fool. But he kept building. He knew what was coming. And we know too.

There is a growing denial of the Hereafter. Even among those who, when asked, declare their belief in the Hereafter, their deeds say something else. The essence of *dhikr*, then, is to remember that we're on a ride that has a definite destination.

There are important supplications that one should say everyday. One of my teachers said that if you are not in the habit of making supplication, then at least say the following everyday: "I seek refuge in the perfect words of God from the evil in what He created." According to a hadith, if one says this in the morning and the evening, three times each, there will be protection from harm or evil that day. There is the famous story of Khālid ibn al-Walīd telling a group of Christians that nothing can harm a person when someone invokes the name of God properly and sincerely. The Christians challenged him to drink poison. Khālid took the poison, as he made the supplication, and no harm came to him.

The next supplication is, "O God, I come to this morning with blessings and well-being and shelter from You, so complete your grace upon me, and [grant me] well-being and shelter in this world and the Hereafter." The Prophet ﷺ said that whoever says this every morning three times has fulfilled his obligation of gratitude for that day.

Next the Prophet ﷺ said that whoever recites the following four times, it is as if he or she has freed a human being from bondage: "O God, I come into the morning bearing witness before You—and before the Carriers of Your Throne, all Your angels, and all of creation—that You are God; there is no God but You alone, without partner, and that Muhammad is Your servant and messenger."

The Prophet ﷺ repeated a supplication that removes any semblance of hidden idolatry in one's soul: "I believe in God the Magnificent, and I reject any sorcery and idolatry, and I hold fast to the firmest handle which never breaks, and God is all knowing, all wise." It is said that this *firm handle* is the Qur'an and the model (or *sunnah*) of the Prophet ﷺ.

Next, the Prophet ﷺ said whoever says the following three times will gain the pleasure of God the Exalted: "I am content with God as the Lord and with Islam as the religion, and with Muhammad ﷺ as the Prophet and the Messenger."

The Prophet ﷺ said we should say seven times in the morning and the evening: "God suffices me. There is no God but Him; on Him do I rely, and He is the magnificent Lord of the throne."

As mentioned previously, asking God to bless the Prophet ﷺ (known as "prayers on the Prophet") is a very beloved act of devotion. We know from a hadith that the Angel Gabriel عليه السلام gave glad tidings to the Prophet ﷺ: whoever says prayers on the Prophet ﷺ, God will requite the worshipper with a similar prayer from Himself, which is a great *raḥmah* (mercy). God the Exalted bestows ten measures of His divine mercy when one says a prayer on the Prophet ﷺ. If one says prayers on the Prophet ﷺ ten times, God the Exalted will bestow 100 measures of His mercy. It is preferable to say this 100 times in the morning and 100 times in the evening. ʿUthmān was known to repeat it 5,000 times a day.

The Prophet ﷺ also prayed, "O God, I ask You for good surprises, and I seek refuge in You from bad surprises."

The Prophet ﷺ said that the best way to seek forgiveness is to say:

"O God, You are my Lord; there is no God but You. You created me and I am Your servant. And Your covenant and promise I uphold to the best of my ability. And I seek refuge in You from the evil of whatever I have done. I acknowledge that all my blessings are from You. And to You I bring my sins, so forgive me because no one can forgive sins but You."

When one faces a calamity or affliction, he or she should say, "What God wills comes to pass, and what He does not will, does not. There is no might or power except with God." And then, "I know that God is powerful over all things, and that God encompasses all things in knowledge." And, "O God, I seek refuge in You from the evil of my soul and the evil of every creature whose forelock You take hold of. My Lord is on the straight path."

These supplications are affirmations of God's oneness and our dependency upon Him and no one else. We call on Him with His excellent names: "O Ever-Living, Sustainer, I seek succor through Your mercy, and I seek safety from Your punishment. Rectify all of my affairs and do not leave me to my own self or to anyone from Your creation even for a blink of an eye."

These supplications affirm our need for safety, mercy, deliverance, and well-being—all of which come from God. A believer strives to affirm these realities through the medium of verbal declarations that, when spoken, connect with unseen dimensions of existence, reaching ultimately to God the Exalted. It is an immensely wise part of the belief system of Islam that we repeat our beliefs so that they never diminish in our hearts nor wane in their meanings.

Jaʿfar al-Ṣādiq said once to a devout atheist, "Have you ever been on the sea?" The atheist told him of one time when he was on a ship during a storm that tore apart his ship and drowned the sailors on board. "I was left clinging to a board. Then the ocean took the board from my hands, and I was left with nothing. An ocean wave then carried me to the shore, and I survived." Jaʿfar said, "When you first boarded the ship, did you place trust in that ship? Didn't the sailors also? Then God took those away from you; then you put your trust in that plank. And when you lost that plank, where did you place your trust? Did you hope that you would survive?" The man told him, "Yes, I did have hope." Jaʿfar al-Ṣādiq said, "There must be an object of hope. Who did you hope for?" The man didn't know how to answer. So Jaʿfar told him, "The one who took away all your means and saved you despite them—that was God."

Even believers become complacent about where they place their trust. We often trust the material things around us, the shelter, the stream of paychecks, cupboards full of food, and so on. We can forget that all of this can be swept away, leaving us with the realization of our only true dependency. How many times have we seen storms take away everything from people: their homes, cars, clothing, and savings?

There is an overriding religious ethic in Islam whose truth is self-evident. If people are serious about living the covenant with God—a more solemn activity does not exist—then there is no choice but to keep our trust in God alive and to affirm our faith and belief in Him. This is not an activity for one day of the week or special sacraments performed a few times a year. This is not the way humans were made. We require a constant and conscious connection with God the Exalted. Supplication is an excellent way to enliven our spiritual growth. When we ask of God, we should do so with trust and certainty that God will answer it. Never should we supplicate with a lazy mind, distracted heart, ceremonial speech, or tone of sanctimony. Heartfelt supplication is far more efficacious. These formulas of *dhikr* and supplication have impact. The authentic testimonies of people receiving blessings from God in the wake of making these heartfelt prayers are numerous.

One should also say, "O God, I seek refuge in You from worry [*hamm*] and grief [*ḥazan*], and I seek Your protection from infirmity and sloth. And I seek refuge in You from cowardice and miserliness, and I seek refuge in You from the stress of debt and from being tyrannized by men." *Hamm* is worry for what may come in the future, while *ḥazan* is grief over what has transpired in the past. This supplication, then, is seeking God's protection from the past and from the future, which to God the Exalted are the same, since He is not limited by time or our perceptions of linear time. Infirmity (*ʿajz*) is not having the ability or power to do something because of some disability. Sloth (*kasl*), however, is having the ability but not the desire, the will, or the drive. Cowardice (*jubn*) is lacking the courage to be firm when firmness is needed, while miserliness (*bukhl*) is cowardice with regard to money. The miser hoards his money out of fear and greed. *Cowardice* and *miserliness* are paired here because each refers to a lack of resolve to strive with the body and wealth. *Debt* and *tyranny are* put together because having debt makes a person beholden to the lender; he or she is enslaved if the lender is unprincipled. On a global level, international debt is a means by which powerful nations keep weaker ones bonded. Economic bondage is a world weapon. There is great wisdom in seeking refuge from debt and being weak before people, for the two go together.

Next there are many supplications of the Prophet ﷺ that ask for well-being (*ʿafiyah*). Scholars have said that after asking for guidance to Islam, one should ask for well-being in spiritual, physical, economic, and social affairs. "O God, I ask You for pardon, well-being, and constant safety in my religion, worldly affairs, family, and possessions."

Next is the supplication, "O God, cover my nakedness [or shame] and assuage my fears." All of us have aspects about ourselves (or of our past) that we regret and hope never bring us shame. Here we ask God, the Knower of the seen and the unseen, to cover our shame and not to humiliate us. Also, none of us is without some kind of fear. Fear has a way of making people vulnerable to acting irrationally and making terrible mistakes. What we ask for here is that God give us calm in times of fear.

"O God, protect me from before me and from behind me and from my right and from my left and from above me. And I seek refuge in Your greatness from unexpected harm from below me [that undermines me]." This comprehensive prayer seeks protection from all directions, literally and metaphorically. This prayer includes seeking protection from the cunning of Satan and his minions. We know from the Qur'an that Satan vowed to accost the Children of

Adam from all sides. *Then I shall come upon them from before them and from behind them and from their right and from their left. And You will not find most of them thankful* (QUR'AN, 7:17).

"O God, You have created me, and You have guided me, and You provide me with food and You provide me with drink. And You shall cause me to die and You cause me to live."

"We have risen this morning on the original pattern of Islam, on the word of sincerity, on the religion of the Prophet Muhammad ﷺ, and on the creed of our father Abraham, who was upright, a Muslim, and not an idolater."

"O God, by Your leave we have come to this morning and by Your leave we have come to the evening, and by Your will we live and by Your will we die. And to You is the ultimate gathering."

"We have come to this morning and the entire dominion has come to this morning belonging to God. And all praise is for God, Lord of all the worlds."

"O God, no blessing has come to me this morning or to anyone else in Your creation but that it is from You alone. You have no partner. All praise and gratitude is due to You for that."

There are additional supplications that one could say, including testimonies of God's glorification and praise, if one has the time. The above supplications should be said everyday. At first it may take time, but once they are memorized they can be said quickly. They are shields of protection—great words associated with blessings.

When these supplications are said each day, you will see the difference in your life. If you skip a day, you will feel a subtle sense that something is missing or incomplete, as if you left home without clothing. First and foremost we should form this habit for the sake of God, for He commanded us to remember Him—the benefit of which is entirely ours. Sīdī Aḥmad Zarrūq said that engaging in regular remembrance is expressing gratitude to God.

It has been a long-standing tradition of the Muslim world that people have some kind of daily devotions beyond the obligatory rites. Obviously, there has been a decline in this. We have lost our remembrance of God. People are deemed "good" Muslims today only because they perform the daily prayers (which is, of course, necessary). But there was a time when neglecting prayer was nearly impossible. There were strong, positive social pressures to perform the prayers.

In Islam, the morning is a time of *sakīnah* (calm and tranquility). Our current culture of "rush" harms our sense of "day" and causes us to miss opportunities of spiritual growth. Speed has become the chief premium: fast food, fast cars, fast rails, fast jets, fast entertainment, and the like. So much speed, but where is it all leading? People have little time to even stop and ask that question. Haste, it is said, is Satan's work. So take time with God, be with Him, in the morning and evening. No one is suggesting the life of a hermit. But do take time to purify the soul and protect it from the mirages and delusory things of modern living.

There is a difference of opinion about making supplications and *dhikr* in groups. Imām Mālik considered it to be reprehensible, though not forbidden outright. He maintained that there was no precedent of this in the actions of the Prophet ﷺ or his Companions. Imam al-Shāfiʿī deemed it to be permissible based on a weak hadith in which the Prophet ﷺ came across a group engaged in congregational *dhikr* but did not stop them. There is also the sound hadith in which angels travel the earth seeking out circles of believers engaged in the remembrance of God. Some scholars believe that it is permissible to have group *dhikr*, but not in unison, that is, not all speaking in one voice. Others say there is no prohibition in speaking with one voice.

The point is: remember God. The Prophet ﷺ told his Companions that the remembrance of God is the best of deeds, greater than *jihad*. Obviously, if one must defend himself, then this *jihad* becomes necessary. But *jihad* is a means, not the end. We were created to remember God.

Appendix Two

Ramadan and Purification

The month of Ramadan is a special time for purifying oneself, the greatest opportunity to implement the discussions and cures with regard to the heart. In fact, this is the purpose, blessing, and secret of the month. It is a remarkable event when the new moon of Ramadan is sighted, when eyes aim toward the horizon shortly after sunset and wait until suddenly a small sliver appears. Qāḍī Abū Bakr ibn al-ʿArabī said in his commentary that the secret of Muslims following a lunar calendar as opposed to a solar calendar is that the sun is used for worldly benefits while the moon is used for *other-worldly* benefits. Witnessing the new moon is seeing *emergence*, as it is known in philosophy. The crescent suddenly emerges in the sky seemingly out of nothing. The reason the moon is not visible at first is because the sunlight is too strong. But as sunset progresses, the light diminishes on the horizon and the sunlight against the crescent itself becomes distinguished from the surrounding crimson sky. So what we actually see of the moon is the sun's light reflected against the lunar sliver. In fact, anything that we see in creation is due to reflected light. And all light comes from God. Witnessing the birth of the new moon is pregnant with metaphor. The word *hilāl* (crescent) is closely related to an Arabic word that refers to birth *(istihlāl)*. So what we see is actually the birth of reflected light. Witnessing the emergence of the new moon is a movement from *ʿilm al-yaqin* (sure knowledge) to *ʿayn al-yaqīn* (direct sure knowledge). The former corresponds to *hearing* a report from another, instead of witnessing the event in person. Imām al-Ghazālī gives the example of a trustworthy person reporting that there is a fire in the forest. This is different from seeing the fire itself, which is *ʿayn al-yaqīn*, a higher sense of awareness, a direct witnessing that requires no report. But to actually touch the fire, thus affirming its reality and precluding visual illusion, this augments one's level of cognisance. This is known as *ḥaqq al-yaqīn* (true sure knowledge). It is related by Imām al-Ḥakim that the Prophet ﷺ said, "The best of God's servants are those who are vigilant about the new moon and shadows to determine the prayer times, as a way of remembering God."

In his poem, Imām Mawlūd went through many of the diseases of the heart. He spoke first about miserliness (*bukhl*). And what better time than Ramadan to shed this malady! It is well known that the Prophet ﷺ was the most generous of people, and in Ramadan he was even more generous. His Companions described him as a wind that bears gifts. Then there is *baṭar*, being gleeful and overjoyed with the fleeting things of this world. The person who fasts during Ramadan experiences an ever greater joy, one related to this world (the happiness of breaking the fast at dusk) and one related to the Hereafter (the ultimate joy of meeting God and receiving lasting bliss of Paradise). We know from sound tradition that God keeps secret the great reward that awaits those who dutifully fast and do so with excellence. There is great disparity between joy in material things and joy in the everlasting acts that survive one's death and accompany them in the next life.

Bughḍ (dislike or hatred) is something more easily eliminated in Ramadan than at other times. The Prophet ﷺ said that the best charity in Ramadan is setting things right between people who are in conflict, even those who harbor hatred for each other. Oppressing or wronging others (*baghḍ*) is anathema to the ethic and spirit of this great month. Ramadan is about gaining position and status with God the Exalted. Moreover, fasting is an act of worship that outwardly cannot be seen in a person.

Love of the world is a disease that we wean ourselves of during Ramadan, for we voluntarily deprive ourselves of the pleasures of food, drink, and sexual intimacy. Love of praise is likewise struck down because Ramadan is a time in which we examine our shortcomings and build resolve and momentum to rectify them. For example, if we are remiss with regard to certain rites of worship, like the Night Prayer vigil (*Qiyām al-Layl*), we ride the momentum of the devotional prayers of *Tarawīḥ* and *convert* them to *Qiyām* after Ramadan passes. The same applies with paying charity, which is especially meritorious during Ramadan.

It is difficult to have ostentation *(riyā')* in Ramadan for a number of good reasons. Ritual prayer is a conspicuous act, as is the Pilgrimage and even paying Charity *(Zakāt)*. Fasting, however, because it involves abstinence, is invisible. One can stare a person in the face and not know whether or not he or she is fasting, which makes fasting an impossible act to flaunt before others. Also, because many people attend the mosque in Ramadan to perform extra devotional prayers, a person prone to ostentation no longer feels so significant. You are one face among hundreds of faces. Ramadan is a time to break habits, which we do when it comes to breaking from consuming food and drink.

Being displeased with the *qadr* (divine decree) of God is a disease fueled by a lack of *imān*, that is, trust and faith in God. Ramadan is a time in which one grows his or her *imān* through the power of voluntary deprivation and patience. When one's *imān* grows, so too does one's understanding and acceptance of what God has decreed.

Rapidly, months pass before our eyes until again Ramadan is upon us. The first days may seem stretched, but thereafter they dash by. Having realization of the movement of time is part of the Ramadan project. To believe that one has a lot of time left in life is what Imām Mawlūd (and many before him, most notably Imām al-Ghazālī) refers to as *long hopes*, foolishly investing all of one's hopes for salvation for some distant date, as if we are guaranteed to live that long.

Bad omens and superstitions can be found in all societies and cultures. It is amazing how millions of people throughout the world make decisions based on what they perceive to be bad omens. Imām Mawlūd mentioned that the cure for this is simply to ignore these superstitions and, in fact, confront them without giving any thought about their ascribed powers. Hunger has a way of dropping the veils on a lot of things, including superstitions. When one experiences hunger, he realizes his utter dependency on God the Exalted and that only He provides and withholds; nothing can bring harm or benefit except by His leave.

Harboring suspicion, rancor, or negative opinions about other people is especially noxious in Ramadan. The same goes for all forms of cheating, vanity, and irrational anger. Ramadan is a month of remembrance, for we stand long in prayer listening to the Qur'an. As such, heedlessness (*ghaflah*) has little refuge in one's mind and heart, which are busy with the remembrance of God. Being mindful of God and His awareness of what moves in and out of one's thoughts and heart expunges negative feelings.

Boasting and arrogance are starved in this month. How can they survive, while we admit our abject need of God and His generous provision? Who can engage in self-aggrandizing when it becomes plain that all that we have is from God the Exalted and is not some mystic result of our own talents and privilege? Profound dislike of being blamed, the fear of death, and other vices spoken of by Imām Mawlūd rise to the surface during Ramadan so that they can be more easily skimmed off and discarded.

All of these blessings of Ramadan come with the obvious caveat: nothing is automatic. This is not the system that God set in place in our lives and the world in which we live. Without effort and sincere trust, Ramadan can easily be just another 30 days in a year, no special moment. Even for those who fast, who mechanically deprive themselves without striving to reach deep into their souls for spiritual lessons, replenishment, and climbing, the month comes and goes with only the sense of inconvenience and then a celebration at the end. Then life goes on as it did the months of the year before. One cannot help but notice a tragedy in this: God so generously opens portals in time, truly special opportunities for us to grow, learn, and build for our Hereafter, yet people turn away from it with casual notice and perfunctory interest.

Imām al-Ghazālī speaks much about fasting in *Iḥya' ʿUlūm al-Dīn*, in the chapter "The Secrets of Fasting." He says that one of the greatest blessings God has given humanity to protect itself from the plots and clever machination of Satan is the fortress of fasting. It is a believer's shield. We have been shown in many verses of the Qur'an and hadith of the Prophet ﷺ that Satan makes inroads into one's soul through hidden gates. There are two of them by which the human being may be destroyed: *shahawāt* and *shubuhāt*. The former is sensory, relating to excessive pleasure (the stomach, the genitals, and all the corollary things that go with that). *Shubuhāt* relates to the heart, which is where Satan works first to create doubt and skepticism about what God has revealed and, in fact, about God Himself. (Satan has far less concern for the deeds of idolaters, those who believe in a multiplicity of gods, or taint their monotheism with attributes that are wholly unbecoming of God the Exalted.)

To lure the believer into doubt is Satan's game. To protect oneself from this is a personal responsibility. We are explicitly told that Satan's guile is weak (QUR'AN, 4:76) and that he has no authority except over those who choose to make themselves vulnerable and who are deluded (QUR'AN, 15:22, 16:99). So to shield against Satan's whisperings, one must guard one's creed and sound belief, and shun shady devices. This entails conforming one's worship with the *sunnah* or established practice of the Prophet ﷺ. It requires deepening one's knowledge in Islam and its various sciences.

If Satan sees that he cannot assail one in matters of creed and belief, he then comes through the door of *shahawāt*, lust and desire. Our desires are integral parts of normal creation and function. But when they evolve into masters that we consciously or unconsciously serve, this is a problem that can become severe enough to drag us outside the fold of guidance. For Satan, this door can be lucrative, especially with consumers of media who receive a steady stream of messages that make licentiousness and excessiveness appear normal. The Prophet ﷺ, told his Companions to be wary of Satan and his designs, for he flows in man's veins. Just as alcohol flows in the blood delivering its debilitating effects to the brain, liver, and other organs, so too do Satan's machinations and enticements.

The Prophet ﷺ said that fasting is half of patience, and patience is a quality indispensable for a successful life and Afterlife. Satan traffics impatience and despair, while fasting exposes the folly of both. The scholars of spiritual purification advise this: be patient with regard to food, which is the primary urge, and with regard to sex, which is the secondary urge. Conquer these two, the rest becomes easy. There is another hadith stating that patience is half of *imān* (faith). So fasting is a quarter of *imān*. There is yet another hadith stating that God the Exalted multiplies the reward for a good action ten to 700 times, except for fasting, "Fasting is My own and I shall reward it," which indicates the enormity of the reward for proper fasting. God says, *Those who are patient shall be rewarded without measure* (QUR'AN, 39:10). Fasting and patience are deeply related; patience too is an important key to the opening of favors from God.

The Messenger of God ﷺ swore that the breath of a fasting person is more pleasing to God than the fragrance of musk. This is enough to know the expanse of the treasure-house of fasting. It is said that the sleep of a fasting person is worship; this is because his fast continues whether he is awake or asleep. This, obviously, does not apply to any other act of worship. Also, when Ramadan comes, the gates of Paradise are open, the doors of Hell are closed, the devils are locked up, and a caller calls from the angelic realm, "O seeker of good, come in this month, and O seeker of evil, cease."

With regard to the verse, *Eat and drink [in Paradise] with full content for what you had done in the days gone by* (QUR'AN, 69:24), Imām al-Shafiʿī says that these bygone days refer to those spent fasting. This is, perhaps, the great lesson of Ramadan, training the soul to forsake temporary sacrifice for a reward that far exceeds the measure of what we do. The sign of sound rational strength is putting off short-term pleasure for a greater long-term pleasure.

It is important to realize also that taking control of our desires defeats Satan. More than a dozen times the Qur'an gives notice that Satan is an avowed and open enemy to humanity who seeks to divert people from God's path and send them spiraling down to debasement in this life and the next. One very important armament against Satan is fasting, which shuts a door through which Satan attacks men and women. And God says, *If you help God, He will help you and make your foothold firm* (QUR'AN, 47:7). Of course, God the Exalted is not in need of any help per se. What "help" here means is actually helping oneself through such immensely beneficial acts as fasting, which vanquish one's caprice and control one's desires. Fasting for religious purposes is becoming increasingly alien in "pleasure societies," where the pursuit of worldly pleasure is so inordinately emphasized.

In a well-known hadith, the Prophet ﷺ said that during Ramadan devils are locked up. Why, then, do we still have bad thoughts? It is a common question. Scholars say that these thoughts originate from our own souls battered by satanic whisperings and devices implanted in us. Another blessing of Ramadan now becomes apparent. It is a time to see what has happened to our soul, what condition it is in, and take notice of our shortcomings: jealousy, envy, overzealous competition, love of gossip, and the rest. During Ramadan, these traits become clear, and a clear enemy is easier to defeat than a slinking one.

Imām al-Ghazālī says that there is an outward and inward fasting. The outward pertains to making sure that the basics are observed, namely, abstaining from consuming anything or having sexual intimacy with one's spouse. The inward is about making sure that the fast is acceptable to God. The Prophet ﷺ, said that there are many people who fast but gain nothing from it except hunger and thirst. Outwardly, their fast seems fine, but inwardly they break their fast with such things as backbiting, lustful glances, lies, and other violations of the inward fast.

There are three types of fasting: the general fast, elect fasting, and fasting of the elect of the elect. The general fast involves preventing the stomach and genitals from fulfillment from dawn until dusk. This is something any Muslim can do. Fasting of the elect involves protecting the eyes, ears, tongue, hands, stomach, genitals, and feet against sin, small or large. Ibn al-Qayyim said that the body of the human being is like a country, whose capital is the heart and whose frontiers are the seven limbs. Satan reaches the heart through one or more of these appendages. Fasting guards the boundaries and trains its sentinels so the heart has a greater chance of drawing near to God.

The word *mu'min* (believer) comes from the same root as *amānah*, which signifies trustworthiness, in which one fulfills a trust he has been given. It is said that one has no *imān* (faith) if he has no *amānah*, that is, if he cannot keep trusts. God Himself, however, has given us trusts: our sight, hearing, and the heart itself, which generates the actions of the other limbs, are all trusts for which we are responsible

(QUR'AN, 17:36). It has also been revealed that on the Day of Resurrection the only currency accepted will be a *sound heart*—not wealth or sons (QUR'AN, 26:89). A sound heart is one protected and nurtured. Likewise, *Whoever pollutes [the soul] has jailed* (QUR'AN, 91:10). We know that the soul and the heart are trusts given to each human being. In fasting, God the Exalted is teaching us how to honor our trusts. Our tongues should be free of slander, lies, backbiting, abominations, and the like; our ears free of hearing the forbidden; our eyes free of lustful glances and other forbidden matters; our hands free of doing anything illicit, like stealing; our feet free from going anywhere prohibited; our genitals free from penetrating or receiving what is not permissible; and our stomachs free from imbibing or consuming forbidden and unwholesome food or drink or consuming in excess. These are trusts we must protect, and an indispensable method of protecting them is through fasting.

Imām al-Ghazālī says the higher form of fasting—the fasting of the elect of the elect—is the fasting of the heart from low aspirations or from worldly thoughts or gains. Ramadan is known as the month for spending for the sake of God—divesting oneself from material assets for the purpose of investing in the Hereafter. In the other months, we are busy acquiring wealth, while in Ramadan we are in the Hereafter-mode of thinking.

One of the scholars of Andalusia said the first degree of *wilayah* (saintliness) with God is to take one's thoughts into account, that is, to measure one's thoughts according to the scale of the *Sharīʿah* (Islamic Sacred Law). Ramadan is the perfect time to take account of the lingering whisperings of the heart and mind. In Arabic, *ʿāmīy* (pi. *ʿawām*) refers to someone whose concern is in such things as the marketplace, which is a metaphor for worldly attachment. It is important to rise above that, to transcend. There are scholars who think that because they are learned, they are not among these *ʿawām*. But this is not always true. There are street sweepers who know only the minimum of their religious obligations and only a few passages from the Qur'an, but their hearts are with God, while there are learned people who are worldly in their ambitions.

Imām al-Ghazālī said, "How many people are not fasting, but with God they are fasting? And how many people are fasting, but with God they are not fasting?" In other words, there are people who, throughout the year, guard their eyes, ears, tongues, genitals, feet, hands, and stomach from corruption. In reality, they are fulfilling the purpose of fasting. Yet there are people who fast physically but with God they are not fasting in that they are not vigilant regarding the unseen aspects of their character and thoughts. When Imām al-Ghazālī speaks about the elect worshippers, he does not merely mean those who are known for their learnedness.

Imām Muḥammad ibn Saḥnūn conducted regular teaching sessions. One day a man came to one of his sessions, walked through the gathering, whispered in the Imām's ear, and then departed. He did this for many days straight, to the point that the Imām asked his students to leave a path for this man to make his way to him. One day the man stopped coming, and Imām Saḥnūn asked about his whereabouts, but the students had no idea why the man stopped coming and why he had been coming in the first place. The Imām then asked someone to find him. When he was brought to the Imām, he asked, "You stopped visiting me. Why?" The man said, "I am a poor man with daughters to marry. Some people who envy you offered me money if I would disturb you every day. And if I were able to make you angry and humiliate you in front of your students, they would reward me so that I can marry my daughters. But when I saw that I had no effect on you, I gave up." The Imām told him, "Why didn't you just ask me for some money?" This is the training of fasting, patience even in the face of insult.

The Companion Salmān al-Fārisī once was a Zoroastrian. He saw the elders of that faith lighting their sacred fire whenever it became extinguished. In fact, Salmān's father was one of the men in charge of keeping the flame. The elders would tell the flock that the flame miraculously kept ablaze no matter what. But Salmān knew of the canard. He went out searching for the truth and came upon a Christian monk with whom he spent some time. He saw him, however, stealing public money and burying it in his yard. So Salman left and came across another monk, who he found to be quite honest. The monk told Salman that the time had come for a prophet to appear in Yathrib and that he should migrate there. Salman was a seeker imbued with great patience, which is key to spiritual wayfaring.

The patience of the Prophet ﷺ was peerless, given all that he had gone through, all the tribulation that he faced. If we do not learn patience from the act of fasting, then we have missed something about this great rite of worship.

Scholars throughout the ages recommended that in order to get the most from Ramadan one should not engage in excessive speech. This is an Islamic ethic that should be practiced in general. But in Ramadan, it is especially advised to be vigilant about what we say, since higher fasting involves guarding the tongue. Also, it is important to utilize our time well. This is a month that our righteous forebears would beg God to let them witness it six months before it came. And for six months after Ramadan, they would beseech God to accept the worship they performed during the month. This is how they viewed this great month. They wept when it passed, which is hardly the popular reaction of our current day. Ramadan is a merciful portal of time that opens and then closes. And none of us knows whether or not we will see another Ramadan. So seize the moment to gain God's mercy, forgiveness, and salvation. There is no capital more worthy of our concern and effort than this.

Imām al-Ghazālī said that the greatest proof of human deficiency is the fact that when a person does something, shortly thereafter he realizes he could have done better. The scholars say use the time, especially the night. Reserve a portion of it to read the Qur'an and stand in prayer. This is, of course, in addition to the *Tarawīḥ* Prayers. The Night Prayer vigil, even if short, is packed with goodness. If it is at the end of the night, then perhaps it is better to recite the shorter sūras, especially those that are associated with special benefits, like the closing verses of Sūrat al-Baqarah (sūrah 2), Sūrat al-Zalzalah (sūrah 99), and others. Also perform the Midmorning Prayer (*Ḍuḥā*), which is performed after the full rising of the sun and before the sun reaches its zenith. One may pray two, four, six, or eight *rakʿahs*. This is a prayer that the Prophet ﷺ did regularly. If one establishes these additional acts of worship during Ramadan, they may be carried over throughout the year, spreading the benefit of Ramadan through the other months.

Also, performing the prayers on time is considered a very important aspect in "establishing prayers" as the Qur'an reminds several times. We all know how tempting it is to delay the prayer to its last possible moment. The obvious problem with this is that it can easily lead to neglecting the prayer altogether. Imām Mālik in his *Muwaṭṭa'* said, "The most important of all your affairs are your prayers. Whoever guards it and is vigilant about its times, he has guarded his religion. And whoever is negligent therein, he is negligent about all the other affairs in his life." It is reported that near his death, the Prophet ﷺ said, "The prayer. The prayer." So prayer is everything. There is no spiritual life without it.

Also know that the time between late afternoon and sunset is a special time for *dhikr* (remembrance of God). ʿAṣr time (when the sun starts its decline) is the signaling of the end of yet another day we have been blessed to see. It is a time of contemplation of the metaphor it represents, the decline of our lives, with sunset signifying the end of a lifetime. So it is a time to remember God and reach out for His mercy. In this culture, however, people see the end of the day as an opportunity for entertainment. Taverns call it "happy hour," when people go to drink and willfully become oblivious of life's purpose.

As the Prophet ﷺ stated, there are two joys associated with fasting. One is the joy of breaking the fast, and the other is when one meets his Lord. Scholars make the analogy that breaking the fast is like meeting our Lord.

It is best to break one's fast as soon as the sun sets. A date, milk, or sip of water would be sufficient. One should then pray the Sunset Prayer (*Maghrib*) before the meal. The time for *Maghrib* is short and goes by quickly. When sunset arrives, break the fast and make the special supplication: "O God, for You I have fasted, and in You have I placed my faith. And I break my fast on Your provision. So forgive me what I have advanced and what I have done, O Lord of the Worlds."

Also, "Gone is the thirst. Moist are the veins. And, God willing, the reward is assured." If you eat at another person's home, offer the following supplication: "May those fasting break their Fasts with you, and may the virtuous eat of your food, and may the angels pray for you."

It is also meritorious to pray in the mosque and to observe the etiquette of being in a place dedicated to worship. One important etiquette is not to engage in idle talk that can deaden the heart. Unfortunately, many people are afflicted with this and do not see their affliction. After the prayer, they linger around and take up senseless conversations. This is not to say that one should not speak at all. It is good to ask one another about health and other matters that show concern and keep love and brotherhood alive. But there should be something meaningful in the discourse.

If we are able to conquer afflictions, such as idle talk and other excesses, we should never belittle people who have yet to do so. We should not don the mantle of a judge and make sententious declarations about others. Instead, thank God for what He has given us. When the Prophet ﷺ saw an affliction in another person, he said quietly, "All praise is for God who granted me well being from what He has tested you with and has favored me above many in creation." It is not arrogance that one recognize a blessing that God has given him or her. Arrogance is when a person feels that he or she especially deserved this blessing. Know that God can take a blessing away and elevate others in rank and honor, even those toward whom people aim their condescension. Once a man falsely accused Muʿādh ibn Jabal of wrongdoing. Muʿādh made supplication against this man. When the man reached old age, he was seen doing unbecoming things to himself and his eyebrows sagged over his eyes. That was a great trial God gave him in his old age for falsely condemning Muʿādh without right.

As mentioned previously, recitation of the Qur'an during Ramadan is especially effective in reviving one's relationship with the Book of God. Imām Abū Ḥanīfah said that reading the Qur'an at least twice a year ensures that one is not estranged from the Qur'an or withdrawn from it. There is a verse in the Qur'an in which the Prophet ﷺ complained that the people have neglected the Qur'an (25:30), that is, they say what is untrue about it or dismiss it. Imām al-Qurtubī says with regard to this verse that on the Day of Resurrection the Qur'an will bear witness against those who neglect it, even those who have learned it but who stopped giving it proper attention. If one is unable to recite, then one should listen to a recording of the Qur'an. For those who are up to it, there is a seven-day litany of completing the Qur'an: the first day, one reads the first three sūrahs; the second day, the next five sūrahs; the third day, the next seven sūrahs; the fourth day, the next nine sūrahs; the fifth day, the next eleven sūrahs; the sixth day, the next thirteen sūrahs; and the seventh day, the remaining sūrahs.

Throughout the centuries, scholars have written much about Ramadan. It truly is an exceptional opportunity to cleanse our hearts of the diseases presented in this volume. Of course, the remedies Imām Mawlūd speaks of can be applied anytime. But during the month of miracles—when the Qur'an itself was revealed—small good deeds are magnified and large deeds multiplied over and over again.

Appendix Three

Aḥmad Zarrūq

Sidi Ahmad al-Zarruq was a great scholar from Morocco who died in 1492. One of the seminal things he said was that the fragrance of his teaching would disseminate in the world long after his bones were laid to rest. It is one of his *karamāt*, or saintly miracles, that his teachings are still alive and still enlighten many people around the world. May God be pleased with him. He offered the following:

> May God give you and us success and rectify our worldly and other-worldly lives and grant us adherence to the way of the truth in our journeys and in our sojourns. Know that repentance is a key, *taqwā* (God-consciousness) is vast, and uprightness is the source of rectification. A servant is never free of either blunders or shortcomings or lassitude. Therefore, never be neglectful of repentance, and never turn away from the act of returning to God the Exalted, and never neglect acts that bring you closer to God the Exalted. Indeed, whenever one of these three occurs, then repent and return to God in penitence.
>
> Every time that you make a mistake, listen and obey. Anytime you display shortcomings or show lack of enthusiasm, do not desist in your efforts. Let your main concern be to remove from your outer state anything that is displeasing, then maintain this state through continual counsel. Persist in doing this until you find that your fleeing from anything outwardly displeasing is second nature and that your avoidance of the boundaries of prohibited things becomes a protective mesh that is placed before you. At this point, it is time to turn inward toward your heart's presence and to its reality, by way of reflection and remembrance. Do not hasten the end result before you have completed the beginning. But likewise, do not begin without looking toward the end result. This is because the one who seeks the outset at the end loses providential care, and the one who seeks the end at the outset loses providential guidance. Act in accordance with principles and the appropriate legal rulings, and not in accordance with stories and fantasies. Do not even consider

stories of how things went with others except as a tonic to strengthen your resolve. Indeed, do not take them as a reference based upon their outward forms or what they seem to be telling us. In all of this, depend upon a clear path you can refer to and a foundation that you can rely on in all of your states. The best of these is the path of Ibn ʿAṭā'allāh, given that it is a clear direction to God. Do not take from the words of others unless it is in accordance with your own path, but submit to their implications if you desire realization. Avoid all forms of vain and foul speech to your absolute utmost. Put aside anything whose benefit you cannot discern immediately. Beware of being extremely hard on your soul before you have obtained mastery over it. But also beware of being too lax with it in anything that concerns sacred rulings. This is because [the soul] constantly flees from moderation in everything, and it inclines towards extremism in matters of both deviance and guidance.

Seek out a companion to help you in your affairs, and take his counsel concerning matters that occur from both your inward states and outward affairs. If you do indeed take his companionship, then treat him in a manner commensurate with his state and give him of your counsel based upon his inabilities and abilities, for the perfect friend is no longer to be found. Indeed, in these times, even a suitable companion who is agreeable rarely lasts. And beware of the majority of people in matters that concern your religious and worldly states unless you have ascertained a person has some sound relationship with his Lord based upon a knowledge free of his caprice or love of leadership and based upon a sound intellect free of the pitfalls of hidden agendas. Do not be heedless of the machinations of others or their hidden states. Consider these two from both their origins and their actions.

A person of character and family distinction rarely affects you with other than good. And yet a person of low origins usually disregards you when times become difficult. Be extremely vigilant of the dominant qualities of a given people in any given land and do not be heedless in the divine wisdom in creation, and notice gatheredness and separation. Some of this we have already covered in our book *al-Qawāʿid*, so take a look at it there. Organize your time in a manner appropriate to the time's specific needs using gentleness and toleration and be very weary of either harshness or laxity. This is because too much laxity concerning permissible matters pulls the heart backward in its journey until even a man of resolve ends up looking like a foolish boy. Work for this world as if you will live forever, but work for the next life as if you will die tomorrow. Thus do not neglect the externals of your worldly needs. In the meantime, do not be heedless of your destiny and final resting place. Be extremely vigilant about avoiding positions of leadership, but should you be tried with such matters at least know your own limitations. Be absolutely sincere with God with the sincerity of one who knows full well who is placing demands upon him. Surrender completely to His decree with the submission of one who knows he can never overcome Him. Have a firm foundation for all of your affairs, and you will be safe from their pitfalls. Organize your devotional practices and you will find your time is extended due to the *barakah* (blessings) in it. Never be fanatical about anything, whether it regards the truth or falsehood; this way your heart will remain in a state of soundness towards others. Never claim anything you are entitled to, let alone what you are not entitled to. This way you will be safe from tricks and treachery. This is because anyone who claims some rank above his own will fall in humiliation, whereas those who claim a rank they warrant will have it stripped from them. But those who claim a station less than their true rank will be elevated to higher levels than they actually deserve. Never give your companion anything of your state other than what his own state warrants. This is because if you descend to his level, he will show you contempt, whereas if you attempt to raise him up to your level, he will abandon you. Never demand a right from anyone, whether one is an intimate or a stranger.

The reason for this is that a stranger in reality owes you nothing, and someone close to you is too precious for you to censure. Never assume that anyone in this world can really understand your circumstances other than from the perspective of his own circumstances. This is because in reality people see things in accordance with their frames of references and their personal paths. However, when aims, purpose, and aspirations are similar, people tend to work together toward a common goal. Never belittle any talk that involves absent people even if there is no harm in it due to the possibility of harm entering into it. Guard your secrets even if you feel safe with someone because the one you divulge your secret to is not a safer place than your own heart from where it emanated. Never leave an atom's weight of your regular devotional practice. Never be lenient with yourself in either lax times or times of high resolve. Indeed, should you miss some practice at a given time, redress it in another time. If you are not able to do your usual practice, at least occupy yourself with something else similar. Never obey your ego even for a moment. Never believe any of its claims no matter what it tells you. Be vigilant about your resolve in all of your affairs to your utmost. In fact, should you resolve to do something, then do it immediately before the resolve wanes. Examine your soul constantly in matters that you are obliged to do or are in need to be done. Anything that you are in no need of doing leave it, even if it is something that is recommended. That means not involving yourself in anything other than absolutely necessary things and real discernible needs. Treat others just as you would want to be treated, and fulfill that which is due to them. All of this is really epitomized in the words of the poet when he said, "If you desire to live such that your religion is safe and your portion is full and your honor is sound, guard your tongue and never mention another's faults remembering that you yourself have faults and others have tongues." Watch your eye. Should it ever reveal to you the faults of others, say to it, "Oh my eye, other people have eyes too." Live treating others well and avoid aggression, and should others aggress against you, leave them but in the best way. The source of these words is in fact none other than the traditions of the Prophet ﷺ when he said, "Be vigilant of God wherever you are, and follow a misdeed with a good deed and it will remove it; and treat others with the most excellent of character." In another tradition the Prophet ﷺ, said, "Every child of Adam errs and the best of those who err are those who seek to redress them." Again the holy spirit inspired my heart's core that no soul will die until it fulfills its decreed portion of this world and its appointed time here. So be conscious of God and make your request with dignity. In summation, repentance, awareness of God, and uprightness are the foundations of all that is beneficial. The truth is clear and its details are weighty and significant. The affair belongs only to God. Success is in His hands.

Qur'an Index

Subject Index

on gratitude, 26
generosity of, 12
on having a good opinion about God, 78, 83
on the Hereafter, 78
on the heart as repository of knowledge, xvi humbleness of, 112,128
on humility, 112
on the importance of silence, 136
love of, 37
on loving to meet God, 76
merciful to his enemies, xx
on miserliness, 13
mocked by people, xv
on moderation, 92-94, 105, 134, 141
on modesty, 37-38
on the natural state of every child, 9
object of scorn and envy, 34
on ostentation, 45-46
on patience, 104
on prayer, 134-135,184
on provisions for people, 68
on remembrance of death, 22,78
on remembrance of God, xiv, 22, 105,151, 171, 191-2
on repentance, 155, 191
on seeking renown, 64
on sincere intentions, xviii
on speaking the truth, 119
on the supplication of the oppressed, 65
on the tongue as interpreter of the heart, 6
on true faith, 3, 19, 131
persecution of by idolaters, xx, 42, 61,98,128
personal strength of, 114
prayers of benediction on, 101, 105-106,152-3
prohibited cursing the world, 24-25
seeing the signs of goodness in people, 82
sent as mercy to the worlds, 94
speaking the truth, 137
supplications of, 49, 60, 71, 86, 102, 122, 135, 148, 159, 162, 166, 169-171, 185
teachings of, 3-4
trials of, 61, 121
universality of, 141
warning against harboring bad thoughts, 82
warning against Satan, 162, 177-178
warning against superstition, 79
witness to humankind, 118
worship practices of, xiv,178

Purification (*Passim*) as a process, 7-9, 140-141

Qarāfī, Imām al-
on hope, 76
on divine decree, 61-62

Qurṭubī, Imām al-
on Qur'an bearing witness in the Hereafter, 186
on ʿUmar ibn al-Khaṭṭāb, 127-128

Qur'an. See *also the "Qur'an* Index"
attributes of God mentioned therein, xvii,163, 164
description of three types of people, xiv
earning a living by the teaching of, 104-105
excellence of the recitation of, 48, 48-9, 79, 101, 106, 106, 148-50,153, 162-163, 183, 185,186
love of, 25
recitation of as remembrance of God, 150, 153, 163-164,
reflection on, 154
teachings of as basis of spiritual purification, xxi, 30

147-148
on caution in trusting people, 82
on consistency in worship, 134
on essence of obedience, 59-60
on *firāsa*, 82
on heedlessness, 64, 66
on ignoring the ignorant, in long excerpt from, 97-100
on the power of truth, 118
on prayers of benediction on the Prophet ﷺ, 106
on regular remembrance of God, 170
on repeating the litany of the Prophet ﷺ 159, 162-171
on wanting Heaven, 51

About the Translator

HAMZA YUSUF WAS born in Walla Walla, Washington. At the age of eighteen, he converted to Islam. Subsequently, he migrated to the Middle East where he spent more than ten years studying Islamic sciences on the Arabian Peninsula and in North and West Africa. He returned to the United States, and during the last twenty years has continued his studies with Shaykh Abdallah bin Bayyah, the foremost living Muslim Jurist in the world.

Hamza Yusuf has also been teaching and writing since his return to the U.S. He has translated into English several classical Arabic texts and poems, including *The Content of Character*, a collection of ethical sayings of the Prophet Muḥammad ﷺ; *The Burda: The Poem of the Cloak*, a thirteenth century devotional poem considered the most recited poem in the world; *The Creed of Imam al-Ṭaḥāwī*, an early tenth century, unifying creed, which serves as a sound basis for Islamic faith and is the most reliable of the early articulations of Muslim belief; and *The Prayer of the Oppressed*, which includes his translation of Imam Muḥammad b. Nāṣir al-Darʿī's powerful and deeply spiritual supplication as well as Hamza Yusuf's own analysis of the nature of oppression and its impact on societies at large and the individual heart.

Through his numerous lectures and media appearances, Hamza Yusuf has been active in the ongoing public discourse about Islam, nationally and internationally. He is also the co-founder of Zaytuna College, the first Liberal Arts Muslim college in the West.